The Ultimate Liquor-Free Drink Guide

Also by Sharon Tyler Herbst

The New Food Lover's Companion,
  Third Edition
The Ultimate A-to-Z Bar Guide
The Wine Lover's Companion
The New Food Lover's Tiptionary,
  Second Edition
Never Eat More Than You Can Lift
The Joy of Cookies
The Food Lover's Guide to Chocolate
  and Vanilla
The Food Lover's Guide to Meat and
  Potatoes
The New Breads
Cooking Smart
The Food Lover's Companion
Simply Sensational Desserts
Breads

The Ultimate Liquor-Free Drink Guide

More than 325 Drinks
with No Buzz,
but Plenty of Pizzazz!

Sharon Tyler Herbst

Broadway Books | New York

BROADWAY

Broadway Books titles may be purchased for business or promotional use or for special sales. For information, please write to: Special Markets Department, Random House, Inc., 1540 Broadway, New York, NY 10036.

PRINTED IN THE UNITED STATES OF AMERICA

BROADWAY BOOKS and its logo, a letter B bisected on the diagonal, are trademarks of Broadway Books, a division of Random House, Inc.

Visit our website at www.broadwaybooks.com

Library of Congress Cataloging-in-Publication Data

Herbst, Sharon Tyler.
    THE ULTIMATE LIQUOR-FREE DRINK GUIDE: More than 325 drinks with no buzz, but plenty of pizzazz! / Sharon Tyler Herbst.
        p.   cm.
    1. Non-alcoholic beverages.   I. Title.
    TX815.H47   2002
    641.8'75—dc21   2001043163

ISBN 978-0-7679-0506-0

Designed by Ralph Fowler
Illustrated by Jackie Aher

To Ron—
my hero, my heart,
my everything

Acknowledgments

Working on a book is never a solitary endeavor. There are countless people who support such a project in myriad ways, big and small, personally and professionally. A warm and heartfelt thanks to:

Close friends and family, who enthusiastically support me no matter what I do: Kay and Wayne Tyler, Tia and Jim McCurdy, Tyler and Andrew Leslie, Jeanette "Sis" Kinney, Lee and Susan Janvrin, Beth Casey, Leslie Bloom, Lisa Ekus, Daniel Maye, Walt and Carol Boice, Sue and Gene Bain, and Harriet Bell, who came up with the idea for this book.

The Broadway Books family: executive editor Jennifer Josephy, the wise and wonderful guiding light; editorial assistant Laura Marshall, who always has a smile in her voice and an answer for everything; copy editor Sonia Greenbaum, who dots my i's and crosses my t's; proofreader Maureen Clark, consistency expert extraordinaire; and the dozens of behind-the-scenes people who labor tirelessly and without fanfare to make the books from Broadway the best they can be.

Cheers to one and all!

Contents

Introduction

No buzz but plenty of pizzazz—that's what the drinks in this book are all about. *The Ultimate Liquor-Free Drink Guide* contains more than 325 recipes for dazzling alcohol-free drinks the whole family can enjoy. The collection includes everything from milkshakes to mocktails, all designed to please the most jaded palate.

There are cold drinks, hot drinks, and even in-between drinks. Drinks for tea lovers (from Almond Tea Latte to the new rage, Bubble Tea), coffee lovers (Iced Café Crème Brûlée to Frappéccino), chocolate lovers (Chocolate Thunder to Hot White Chocolate) . . . you name it, it's here! There are smoothies, eggnogs, and punches—drinks for one and drinks for bunches. Beat-the-heat treats, including sparkling coolers like Watermelon Whirl and Orange Rush, and a chapter devoted entirely to ades (lemon, lime, orange, and others), all ready to rescue the thirsty.

Those in a virtuous mood will be drawn to the Good-for-You Drinks chapter, complete with a list of energizing nutrition boosters. Those in a mood to be naughty will start grinning just browsing through the chapter on Frosty Pleasers, which includes dozens of decadent concoctions from Chocolate Cheesecake Shake to Frosty Apple Pie à la Mode. Armchair travelers with an adventurous spirit will enjoy the chapter on Drinks from Around the World, with lively libations from destinations ranging far and wide.

This book comprises a lucky thirteen chapters to make your drink search easy. In fact, it is designed to be the ultimate user-friendly guide to alcohol-free drinks. The recipes are simple and none require exotic ingredients or any equipment more complex than a blender. There's a section on how to make great drinks and another with tips on how to create easy, showy garnishes for them. Plus there's plenty of information on drink-making tools and glassware, a table of measurements and their equivalents, a large ingredients glossary, and a chart on ingredient equivalents. In short, everything you need to make show-stopping drinks for any occasion.

So there you have it—more than 325 ways to have fun and create delicious drinks without alcohol, to imbibe by yourself in a hammock or for a party where your drinks are the stars. I hope you have as much fun making them and drinking them as I did creating them!

How to Use This Book

Ingredients are listed first in tablespoons and cups, for home use, and then in fluid ounces, for bartenders looking for zero-proof drinks.

For drinks where such measurements don't apply, yogurt is given in two sizes (6 ounces and 8 ounces) because some flavored yogurts are only sold in 6-ounce cartons.

The term "ice cubes" always refers to the standard size rather than the miniature size.

To facilitate the drink-making process, there are sections on Equipment for Making Drinks (page 4), Tips for Making Great Drinks (page 10), Garnishing Drinks (page 13), Measurement Equivalents (page 18), and Ingredient Equivalents (page 36).

There's an extensive Ingredients Glossary (page 20) in which you'll find definitions for terms that may be unfamiliar to you (such as falernum and Jamaica flowers), as well as informational tidbits on familiar foods, such as eggs.

The book's Index is particularly extensive, listing recipes by the name of the drink, as well as by the drink's primary ingredients.

That's it—now go and have fun with these good libations!

Equipment for Making Drinks

Blender  Drinks like smoothies and shakes require a blender—a food processor can leak and simply won't produce the desired results. A simple three-speed machine with a 2-quart container will do fine. I like a glass pitcher because I can see what's happening inside. Check the manufacturer's instructions before putting whole ice cubes in a blender—some advise against it because doing so can damage the blades. *See also* Ingredients Glossary, Ice, page 28; Blender Techniques, page 12.

Bottle Stopper (for dealcoholized sparkling wines) A special spring-loaded stopper with two metal wings that fold down and over the neck of a sparkling wine or apple juice bottle. It helps retain a sparkler's effervescence for at least 24 hours.

Citrus Reamer *see* JUICE EXTRACTOR

Citrus Spout Also called a *lemon spout*, this great little tool is perfect for when you only want a small amount of juice. It has a covered spout (with a built-in strainer), the opposite end of which is screwed into the stem end of a lemon, lime, or orange. After squeezing out the required amount of juice, the fruit (spout in place) should be wrapped in a plastic bag and stored in the refrigerator until the next use. *See also* JUICE EXTRACTOR/CITRUS REAMER.

Citrus Stripper   A special stainless-steel tool with a notched edge that cuts ¼-inch-wide strips from citrus rinds. Great for making lemon twists (*see* Garnishing Drinks, page 13). *See also* CITRUS ZESTER; VEGETABLE PEELER.

Citrus Zester   A tool specially designed to remove the zest (the outer, colored portion) of citrus fruits. It has a stainless-steel cutting edge with five tiny holes, which create threadlike strips of peel as the tool is drawn across the fruit. *See also* CITRUS STRIPPER; VEGETABLE PEELER.

Cocktail Shaker   *see* SHAKER

Glassware   Sure, it would be nice to have glasses in every shape and size, but it's not very practical for most of us. To make it easy on you, I've limited the types of glasses used for the recipes in this book. Following are some of the styles you might like to have on hand. Rather than specify a "Collins" or "highball" glass, I've kept things simple by calling for a tall glass, which holds 12 to 14 ounces. The short, squat **old-fashioned glass** holds about 6 ounces. The classic flared, long-stemmed **cocktail glass** (sometimes called a *martini glass*) is primarily for drinks without ice and holds anywhere from 4 to 10 ounces—choose a medium size if you're buying new glasses. The tall, slender **champagne flute** holds about 8 ounces and is preferred for drinks like Kir (page 239) and for many sparkling beverages. A medium (8- to 12-ounce) **wineglass** is great for myriad drinks. If you only have room or budget for one style, choose a white-wine glass, which has a more tapered bowl. **Punch cups** hold 6 to 8 ounces—tempered glass cups can be used for both hot and cold punches. **Irish coffee mugs** hold 8 to 10 ounces and are great for all manner of hot drinks.

Ice Cream Scoop   Not a *must,* but extremely handy for making milkshakes and such, and inexpensive enough to add to most repertoires. There are many styles and sizes of ice cream scoops on the market today. The scoop I used for the recipes in this book holds 3 ounces (measure a scoop by filling it with water, then measuring the water).

Ice Crusher Some of us are lucky enough to have a freezer that delivers crushed ice at the push of a button. If you're not one of those people, there are a wide variety of relatively inexpensive ice crushers, from manual crank styles to electric ones. You can find them almost anywhere, from supermarkets to hardware and department stores. *See also* the section on Ice, page 28, in the Ingredients Glossary.

Juice Extractor/Citrus Reamer A must-have for

squeezing fresh juice. There are dozens of styles, ranging from small, handheld reamers, to those that straddle a measuring cup and have a built-in strainer, to electric juicers. *See also* CIT-RUS SPOUT.

Measuring Cups There are two different types of mea-

suring cups. **Dry measuring cups,** used for ingredients like sugar and chopped fruit, typically come in a nested set of 5, ranging from ⅛ cup to 1 cup. **Liquid measuring cups** are made of glass or plastic, and range in size from 1 to 8 cups.

Mixing Glass A large (at least 16 ounces) glass that sometimes has a pouring spout, used for stirring drinks with ice. Any large glass, small pitcher, or even a tall glass measuring cup will do. *See also* SHAKER.

Muddler Typically made of wood because it won't  scratch glass, a muddler has a broad, rounded, or flattened end with which to crush ingredients like mint leaves, as for Mint Julep Tea, page 172. A ceramic mortar and pestle can also be used. Although it will take longer, the same effect can be achieved by muddling with a long-handled wooden spoon.

Shaker Stainless-steel shakers produce colder drinks than those made of aluminum. A standard three-piece "cocktail" shaker comprises the container, a lid with a built-in strainer, and a cap for the lid. A Boston shaker has two halves (one stainless steel, the other glass) that fit together end to end. This shaker requires a coil bar STRAINER to hold back the ice as the drink is poured. *See also* MIXING GLASS; Tips for Making Great Drinks, page 10.

Strainer Some shakers have built-in strainers, but you can use any strainer. The flat Hawthorne bar strainer has a spring coil that fits inside mixing glasses and shakers.

Stripper   *see* CITRUS STRIPPER

Vegetable Peeler   A simple tool found everywhere from
 supermarkets to hardware stores—good for
making wide citrus-peel garnishes. *See also*
CITRUS STRIPPER; CITRUS ZESTER.

Zester   *see* CITRUS ZESTER

Tips for Making Great Drinks

No drink-making challenge will be intimidating once you have a few techniques under your belt. Here are some tips that can make your drinks look and taste outstanding.

Chilling Glasses Cold glasses give drinks a nice cold jump-start. Chill the glasses in the freezer for 10 minutes, or in the refrigerator for 30 minutes. Or pack a glass with crushed or cracked ice and let stand until cold—5 minutes should do it. Discard the ice, shaking out any water before filling the glass with the drink of your choice.

Freezer-Frosted Glasses For a fun, frosty presentation, put the glasses in the freezer an hour ahead of when you want to use them. For an ultrafrosty effect, dip the glasses in cold water, shake off any excess, and place in the freezer.

Frosting Glass Rims with Sugar or Salt Some recipes call for coating the rim of a glass with salt (*see* Margarita, page 240) or sugar (*see* Cosmopolitan, page 238). Just dip the glass rim in water or fruit juice, shake off the excess liquid, then dip the rim into salt (preferably coarse) or granulated sugar that's been poured onto a saucer. The rim can also be dampened by simply dipping your fingertip into a liquid, then running it around the glass rim, or by rubbing the glass rim with a lemon, lime, or orange wedge. Sugar- or salt-frosted glasses may be prepared in advance and stored in the freezer or refrigerator until needed.

Shaking and Stirring Drinks Some drinks (primarily Mocktails, *see* Chapter 12) require either shaking or stirring. The basic guidelines for either technique are: (1) Fill a shaker halfway full with ice, then add the ingredients. (2) Shake or stir a drink long enough to thoroughly chill the ingredients—too long and the drink becomes diluted with the melting ice. (3) Don't let a shaken or stirred drink sit on the ice—immediately strain it into the serving glass. (4) To retain maximum effervescence of a sparkling beverage (like seltzer water), add it after a drink has been shaken or stirred, stirring gently to combine.

Shaking: Don't overfill the shaker—there should be plenty of room for the ingredients and ice to move around. The general rule is two drinks at a time. *Tightly* attach the lid and, holding the shaker with both hands (one on each end), shake it up and down. You may want to wrap the shaker in a towel before beginning because the shaker gets frosty cold. *See also* SHAKER, page 8.

Stirring: A drink can be stirred with ice either in a cocktail shaker or in another narrow container, like a pitcher (*see* MIXING GLASS, page 7). Fill the container halfway full of ice cubes, then add the ingredients. With a long-handled wooden or metal spoon, stir vigorously for 10 to 20 seconds, or long enough for the ice to chill the ingredients thoroughly. Strain the drink into a serving glass.

Blender Techniques Unless the blender manufacturer's instructions say you can use whole ice cubes (which can damage some blades), use crushed ice (*see* Ingredients Glossary, Ice, page 28). Put the drink ingredients in the blender jar first. If you're using pieces of fruit, purée the liquid ingredients and fruit before adding the ice and blending again. Whenever you use the blender, make sure the cover is securely attached before turning on the machine. Start at low speed, gradually increasing to the maximum speed desired. *Particular caution must be taken when blending hot liquids*—hold the lid down securely with an oven mitt–protected hand and *always* start at low speed.

Muddling The word "muddle" simply means to mash or crush ingredients together to release their flavors. This technique is traditionally done with a muddler (see page 8), a special wooden rod with a broad, rounded, or flattened end (available in gourmet and bar-supply stores). The back side of a wooden spoon (a long-handled one if the drink is tall) can be used as well. The most well-known drink that employs muddling is the classic mint julep (*see* Mint Julep Tea, page 172), in which mint leaves and sugar are crushed together.

Garnishing Drinks

Presentation is a big part of life, no doubt about it. Garnishing, although not necessary, gives drinks a finishing touch. Easy garnishes include fruit slices or wedges, carrot curls, grated chocolate, whipped cream, crumbled cookies, candy-stick stirrers, chocolate-covered mints . . . the list is endless. Some sliced fruits—such as apples, bananas, and pears—darken quickly when exposed to the air. Lightly brush these fruits with lemon juice to retard discoloration. Frosty glasses (*see* Freezer-Frosted Glasses, page 10) are another way to create a special look for drinks. Drinking straws are a must for many libations, and tiny paper umbrellas (available at specialty shops and liquor stores) make any drink look tropical. Following are techniques for making easy, decorative garnishes that look and taste great.

Berries Large strawberries and blackberries make a showy garnish. Cut a slit from the berry's tip to within ¼ inch of the stem's end to make a slot for the berry to straddle the glass rim. Smaller berries like raspberries and blueberries may be speared on a decorative pick and rested on the glass rim or dropped into the drink.

Carrot Curls   Use a vegetable peeler to cut thin, wide strips the length of a large carrot. Drop the strips into a bowl of ice water until ready to serve. Blot on a paper towel before using.

Celery Brushes   Cut celery ribs in 2- to 5-inch lengths (depending on how long you want the brush to be). Slit each piece lengthwise at about ¼-inch intervals to within 1 inch of the other end. Place the cut celery in a large bowl of ice water; cover and refrigerate for an hour, or until curled.

Chile-Pepper Flowers   These colorful garnishes are great for drinks like a Virgin Mary, page 249. Choose small, brightly colored chiles—red, green, or yellow. Wear gloves to protect your hands from the chile's volatile oils. Use a sharp, pointed knife to cut each pepper from the tip to the stem's end at about ⅜-inch intervals. Remove the seeds and, if desired, trim the "petal" tips to form points. Place in a bowl of ice water for 1 hour, or until the chile peppers open into flower shapes.

Citrus Spirals   Begin at one end of a lemon (or other fruit) and use a citrus stripper (*see* page 5) to cut around and down the fruit, creating a long, continuous spiral of rind. A sharp paring knife can be used, though it's not as easy to work with.

Citrus Twists   The most simple of garnishes, a twist can be made from any citrus fruit. Cut the twists just before using them so they're as fresh as possible. The easiest way to produce strips is to use a citrus stripper (*see* page 5). Alternatively, you can use a sharp paring knife or vegetable peeler to slice off thin, ½-inch-wide strips of peel. If you're having a party and need lots of twists, do this: Cut off both ends of a lemon, then cut the fruit in half lengthwise and use a grapefruit spoon to remove the fruit, taking as much of the white pith with it as possible. Then cut the rind lengthwise into ¼-inch strips. Before dropping a twist into a drink, hold it at both ends, colored part down, and give it a twist just above the drink's surface. This twisting motion produces an infinitesimal spray of citrus oil into the drink. For additional flavor, rub the glass rim with the peel before twisting.

Fruit, General   Thoroughly wash fruit that will be used unpeeled, such as oranges, lemons, and limes. To keep fruits like bananas, peaches, and apples from darkening, use a pastry brush to lightly coat the cut surface with lemon or lime juice; blot off excess. Fruits with pits, like cherries and apricots, should be pitted before garnishing a drink. Pit cherries with a cherry pitter, or use the tip of a vegetable peeler or a pointed knife. Melon can be peeled and either cut into small wedges or made into balls with a melon baller, available at gourmet shops and some supermarkets.

Fruit Slices (or Wheels)   With a sharp knife or one with a serrated edge, cut fruit (such as oranges, lemons, limes, and bananas) crosswise into ¼-inch-thick slices. Make a cut from the outer edge to the center of the slice to create a slot for the fruit to straddle the glass rim. **For half slices,** cut the fruit crosswise in half, put the flat side down, and cut into ¼-inch slices. Make a cut from the center to the inside edge of the peel to create a notch to hook the fruit over the glass rim.

Fruit and Vegetable Fans Use a sharp, pointed knife to cut the fruit or vegetable (such as a strawberry or a radish) lengthwise into thin slices, slicing to within ¼ inch of the stem's end. For strawberries, with your fingers gently fan out the slices. Drop the radish fans into a bowl of ice water and refrigerate for 1 hour to allow the slices to swell and fan out.

Fruit Wedges Slice the fruit lengthwise in half; cut each half lengthwise into quarters or eighths, depending on the size of the fruit. Make a cut from the center to the inside edge of the peel to hook the fruit over the glass rim.

Scallion Brushes Trim off the root end and most of the green portion of a scallion. Use a sharp, pointed knife to thinly slash both ends at ⅛-inch intervals, leaving a 1-inch uncut space in the center of the scallion. Place in a bowl of ice water in the refrigerator for 1 hour, or until the slashed tips curl. Refrigerate until ready to use. Scallion brushes are fun garnishes for drinks like Gazpachito, page 85.

Scalloped Edges For a scalloped effect for citrus fruits, cucumbers, and so on, use a paring knife or a citrus stripper to cut through the skin in evenly spaced, lengthwise channels at about ½-inch intervals. When the fruit is sliced crosswise, the channels produce a scalloped effect.

Measurement Equivalents

pinch/dash	$\frac{1}{16}$ tsp.
$\frac{1}{2}$ tsp.	30 drops
1 tsp.	$\frac{1}{3}$ Tbsp.; 60 drops
3 tsp.	1 Tbsp.
$\frac{1}{2}$ Tbsp.	$1\frac{1}{2}$ tsp.
1 Tbsp.	3 tsp.; $\frac{1}{2}$ fluid oz.
2 Tbsp.	$\frac{1}{8}$ cup; 1 fluid oz.
3 Tbsp.	$1\frac{1}{2}$ fluid oz.; 1 jigger
4 Tbsp.	$\frac{1}{4}$ cup; 2 fluid oz.
$5\frac{1}{3}$ Tbsp.	$\frac{1}{3}$ cup; 5 Tbsp. plus 1 tsp.
8 Tbsp.	$\frac{1}{2}$ cup; 4 fluid oz.
$\frac{1}{8}$ cup	2 Tbsp.; 1 fluid oz.
$\frac{1}{4}$ cup	4 Tbsp.; 2 fluid oz.
$\frac{1}{3}$ cup	5 Tbsp. plus 1 tsp.
$\frac{3}{8}$ cup	$\frac{1}{4}$ cup plus 2 Tbsp.
$\frac{1}{2}$ cup	8 Tbsp.; 4 fluid oz.
$\frac{2}{3}$ cup	10 Tbsp. plus 2 tsp.
$\frac{5}{8}$ cup	$\frac{1}{2}$ cup plus 2 Tbsp.
$\frac{3}{4}$ cup	12 Tbsp.; 6 fluid oz.
$\frac{7}{8}$ cup	$\frac{3}{4}$ cup plus 2 Tbsp.
1 cup	16 Tbsp.; $\frac{1}{2}$ pint; 8 fluid oz.
2 cups	1 pint; 16 fluid oz.

1 pint. . . . . 2 cups; 16 fluid oz.

3 cups. . . . . 1½ pints; 24 fluid oz.

4 cups. . . . . 1 quart; 2 pints; 32 fluid oz.

1 quart . . . . 2 pints; 4 cups; 32 fluid oz.

2 pints. . . . . 4 cups; 1 quart; 32 fluid oz.

8 cups. . . . . 2 quarts; 64 fluid oz.

4 quarts . . . . 1 gallon; 8 pints

1 gallon. . . . . 4 quarts; 8 pints; 16 cups; 128 fluid oz.

Ingredients Glossary

Every ingredient that goes into a drink affects its flavor, so the first rule of thumb is to use the best you can find. The following ingredients are listed alphabetically.

Alcohol-Free Wines and Beers   *see* DEALCOHOLIZED WINES; NONALCOHOLIC BEER

Butter   For drinks like Cinnamon Toast Toddy, page 192, unsalted butter is preferable to salted butter.

Chocolate   *see* COCOA POWDER; MEXICAN CHOCOLATE

Club Soda   Water that's been highly charged with carbon dioxide, which makes it bubbly. It contains small amounts of sodium bicarbonate and sodium citrate, which give it a slightly salty-citric flavor. Club soda is also called *soda water. See also* SELTZER WATER; TONIC WATER; WATER.

Cocoa Powder, Unsweetened   There are two styles of unsweetened cocoa powder—regular and Dutch process. **Dutch cocoa,** the richer and darker of the two, has been treated with an alkali, which helps neutralize cocoa's natural acidity. Don't substitute cocoa mixes, which contain other ingredients such as milk powder and sugar, for unsweetened cocoa powder.

Coconut Milk   An unsweetened, milklike liquid made by processing water with coconut meat. Coconut milk is commonly available in Asian markets and can be found in many supermarkets (look in the ethnic food section). As with all coconut products, coconut milk is high in saturated fat—select the low-fat version, which delivers the same flavor with fewer calories. Some Asian markets carry a more concentrated **coconut cream,** which is not to be confused with the extremely sweet CREAM OF COCONUT.

Coffee; Coffee Powder   For coffee drinks that are to be iced, use chilled double-strength coffee. The fullest instant coffee flavor comes from instant espresso powder—a good brand is Medaglia d'Oro, available in most supermarkets. If you can't find instant espresso powder, use 1½ times the amount called for of regular instant coffee (crush the granules into powder so they'll dissolve more easily in cold liquids).

Cream of Coconut   A thick, extremely sweet mixture of coconut paste, water, and sugar. Cream of coconut, used in drinks like Tiña Colada (page 248), is commonly available in supermarkets and liquor stores. Always stir well before using, as this mixture separates in the can. *See also* COCONUT MILK.

Dealcoholized Wines Wines produced by one of several special processes that remove the alcohol. Dealcoholized wine—a term preferred by the wine industry, though it can also be called *alcohol-free wine* and *nonalcoholic wine*—is legally a nonalcoholic product, which means it contains less than 0.5 percent alcohol (oddly enough, this is about the same amount in most freshly squeezed orange juice). That in itself makes this product appealing to many, but weight watchers love the fact that dealcoholized wine has less than half the calories of regular wine. And to top it all off, according to *The American Journal of Clinical Nutrition,* nonalcoholic red wine is also good for the heart.

But these nonalcoholic alternatives do not have the subtlety, body, and mouthfeel of real wine, primarily because it is alcohol that contributes to all of those characteristics. Still, there are some good dealcoholized wines on the market in a variety of styles, including reds, whites, rosés, and sparkling wines. You can even find some varietals like Chardonnay, Cabernet Sauvignon, Merlot, and Johannisberg Riesling. However, most tasting panels agree that the simpler styles, such as Ariel Blanc and Sutter Home Fré Premium White, have the best flavor—happily, they're also the least expensive. Among the more popular producers of dealcoholized wines are Ariel Vineyards, Sutter Home Winery (Fré wines), Carl Jung Wines, Inglenook St. Regis, and Meloni Vino Zero. These wines can be found at liquor stores and some supermarkets, and are typically grouped together. For more information on wines without alcohol, see: www.non-alcoholicbeverages.com.

Eggs   The recipes in this book use large grade AA eggs. To prevent a piece of eggshell from getting into a drink mixture, break an egg into a small bowl before adding it to the other ingredients. That way it will be easier to remove any bits of shell that break off. **Separating eggs** is easier if they're cold. An inexpensive egg separator (available in kitchenware stores and some supermarkets) makes separating eggs easy. Or crack an egg into a funnel set over a bowl or cup—the white falls through, the yolk won't. The time-honored method of separating eggs by passing the yolk back and forth from one half of the shell to the other while the white slips into a bowl below is generally fine, but you should know that minute bacteria on the shell's surface might transfer to the raw egg. **Beating egg whites** not only takes less time if the whites are at room temperature, but you'll get more volume out of them. To quickly warm cold egg whites, set the bowl of whites in a larger bowl of warm (not hot) water. Stir occasionally until the whites have reached room temperature.

Are raw eggs safe? Some people declare that raw eggs should never be eaten because of possible salmonella infection. The truth is that the number of affected eggs is relatively small. However, though fairly rare, there have been cases of egg-related salmonella food poisoning in some parts of the United States (primarily the northeastern and mid-Atlantic states). The origin of most cases is commercial establishments (such as restaurants) and is due to improper handling, such as letting preparations containing raw eggs or slightly cooked eggs stand too long at unsafe temperatures. Nevertheless, if you question your egg supply or suffer from a weakened immune system, it's best to *avoid all raw-egg preparations entirely.* Those most susceptible to foodborne illness are pregnant women, people with chronic disease, the elderly, and the very young.

Consumers have at least a couple of alternatives to raw eggs available to them: **Egg substitutes** contain about 80 percent egg whites (and no yolks), the other 20 percent comprising such ingredients as nonfat milk, tofu, vegetable oils, emulsifiers, and coloring. They can be used in recipes that don't depend on the yolk for thickening or require the white to be beaten. **Pasteurized shell eggs** are just that— eggs that have been pasteurized *in the shell.* This process employs water at controlled temperatures, which kills all salmonella strains without measurably altering the raw appearance of the egg. At this writing, only one U.S. company is producing pasteurized shell eggs, which are primarily available along the East Coast and in scattered midwestern cities. Broader availability is expected soon. For more information on pasteurized shell eggs, go to www.davidsonseggs.com or call 603-528-3042.

Evaporated Milk   A canned, unsweetened milk from which 60 percent of the water has been evaporated. Evaporated milk has a slightly caramelized, "canned" flavor and comes in whole, low-fat, and nonfat styles. It can be stored at room temperature. After opening, refrigerate and use within 5 days.

Falernum   [fuh-LER-num] Made in the West Indies, falernum is a syrupy sweetener with a flavor reminiscent of lime, ginger, and almonds. *See also* SYRUPS, FLAVORED.

Flavored Syrups   *see* SYRUPS, FLAVORED

Flowers, Edible   Flowers add an exotic touch to tropical drinks, but you should know that not all flowers are edible, which means they shouldn't touch anything that is. Purchase flowers that have been specifically grown for use with food and drink—they're available at specialty produce markets and some supermarkets. Flowers that have been sprayed with pesticide are a no-no. And before using flowers from your garden (assuming they're pesticide-free), call your local poison control center to make sure they aren't inherently poisonous. Edible flowers include chrysanthemums, daisies, nasturtiums, pansies, roses, and violets.

Fruit, General   Fresh fruit is preferred for making the drinks in this book, although frozen fruit can be used when fresh is unavailable; canned fruit is a last resort.

The flavor of peaches simply doesn't hold up when processed—taste one before adding it to a drink. To make a slushy out of any blended drink, put slices or chunks of fresh fruit on a plate or small baking sheet and pop in the freezer for an hour—just until the fruit is icy but not solid. Frozen fruit quickly loses its texture on thawing, so it isn't suitable for garnishes.

Fruit Juices   There are dozens of fruit juices and nectars in markets today, ranging from single-fruit favorites to exotic combinations. The only types of which I ask (beg, cajole, demand, and plead!) you to use the fresh forms are lemon and lime juices. That's because most packaged versions have an unnaturally acidic edge and some can taste downright nasty. Fresh orange juice is also preferable, although juice made from frozen concentrate is often more flavorful than fresh-squeezed juice.

Tips on juicing citrus fruits:

1. Lemons and other citrus fruits that are heavy for their size will be much juicier than their lightweight counterparts.

2. Room-temperature fruit yields more juice than refrigerated fruit.

3. Before juicing, soften the fruit by using your palm to roll it around on the countertop several times. Or prick the skin in several places with a fork (don't go all the

way through to the flesh); microwave at HIGH (100 percent power), uncovered, for 10 to 20 seconds, depending on the size of the fruit. Let stand 1 minute before rolling the fruit between your palm and the countertop.

4. If you need only a little juice, soften the fruit as previously indicated, then insert a citrus spout (*see* page 4)—a nifty gadget that allows you to extract small amounts of seedless juice.

5. Leftover fresh-squeezed citrus juice can be covered and refrigerated for up to 5 days.

Grenadine [GREHN-uh-deen; grehn-uh-DEEN] A sweet, deep red, pomegranate-flavored syrup that was once made exclusively from pomegranates grown on the Caribbean island of Grenada. Today, other fruit juice concentrates are often used to make this syrup. Most grenadines are nonalcoholic, but check the label, as some contain a small amount of alcohol. *See also* SYRUPS, FLAVORED.

Hibiscus *see* JAMAICA FLOWERS

Honey There are hundreds of different honeys on the market today, most of them named for the blossom from which they originate. In general, the darker a honey's color, the stronger the flavor, though there are exceptions to every rule. Choose a honey that suits your palate. If the honey crystallizes, reliquefy it by placing the opened jar either in a microwave oven at HIGH for 20 to 30 seconds (depending on the amount) or in a pan of hot water over low heat for 5 to 10 minutes. **Honey caveat:** Experts tell us that, because even pasteurized honey can contain heat-resistant botulism spores, it should never be given to children under two years—a group for whom it can be particularly dangerous.

Ice   A drink's flavor can be ruined with off-tasting ice, and ice can taste only as good as the water from which it's made. Ice can easily take on odors from foods in freezing compartments. Sample it before using—if it doesn't taste good, buy packaged ice. Ice cubes are versatile because they can be used as is or crushed.

Ice cubes made with water that's been boiled and cooled will be clearer than those made with regular tap water. *See also* Flavored Ice Cubes, page 261; Decorated Ice Cubes, page 262.

Crushed ice should be used in drinks that call for it— ice cubes won't contribute the right texture for some drinks (such as Cucumber Crave, page 94). Inexpensive manual or electric ice crushers are widely available *(see* page 7). Or you can simply place ice cubes in a heavy-duty plastic bag, seal, then wrap in a heavy towel and whack away with a mallet, rolling pin, or other heavy instrument until the ice is crushed as desired. Prepare crushed ice in advance and store in a plastic bag in the freezer. Remember, crushed ice melts much faster than ice cubes and will dilute a drink more quickly.

Punch-Bowl Ice *see* page 260

Ice Cream Frozen desserts like ice cream, gelato, and sherbet should be slightly softened before adding them to a blended drink mixture such as a milkshake. Either let them stand at room temperature for about 15 minutes, or zap them in a microwave oven at MEDIUM-LOW (30 percent power) for 20 to 30 seconds, depending on the amount. To speed the softening process, scoop out the ice cream and put it on a plate. *See also* Ice Cream—It Could Be a Lot of Cold Air, page 126.

Instant Espresso Powder *see* COFFEE

Jamaica Flowers This red hibiscus family member isn't a flower at all, but the flower's calyx—the portion that covers and protects the bloom before it opens. Dried Jamaica flowers are used in teas (such as Celestial Seasonings' Red Zinger) and to make drinks like Agua de Jamaica, page 40. They can be found in natural food stores (labeled "Jamaica flowers," "hibiscus flowers," or "Roselle") and in Latin markets (called *flores de Jamaica* or simply *Jamaica*). When selecting the flowers, look for those that are brightly colored—dull or dark flowers indicate age and less flavor. Store them airtight in a cool, dry place for up to 1 year. Because the flowers have a high acid content, it's necessary to use a nonreactive container, such as glass or stainless steel, when adding them to a recipe.

Maple Syrup Because of its superior flavor, pure maple syrup is recommended for the recipes in this book. The labor-intensive processing necessary to produce maple syrup makes it more expensive than "maple flavored syrup" (typically corn syrup with a soupçon of maple syrup) or "pancake syrup" (corn syrup flavored with artificial maple extract), but the flavor bonus is well worth the extra expense. Pure maple syrup should be refrigerated after opening.

Mexican Chocolate A sweet, grainy chocolate flavored with cinnamon and sometimes almonds. Mexican chocolate can be found in Latin markets.

Milk, Evaporated *see* EVAPORATED MILK

Milk, Sweetened Condensed *see* SWEETENED CONDENSED MILK

Mixers Store mixers like tonic water, seltzer water, and ginger ale in the refrigerator so they'll be cold when added to a drink. Room-temperature liquids cause ice to melt faster, diluting the drink. Tightly reseal carbonated mixers, refrigerate, and use within 2 to 3 days—after that, they lose their pizzazz.

Nonalcoholic Beer (Brew) A beer with the alcohol removed in one of two ways: either by fully fermenting the product, then removing the alcohol, or by arresting the fermentation before it begins. As with DEALCOHOLIZED WINES, nonalcoholic beer (also referred to simply as *NA*) contains a minuscule amount of alcohol (0.5 percent by volume). That's no more than is contained in many fruit juices, which, thanks to natural fermentation, can have an alcohol level ranging between 0.2 and 0.5 percent. Although such potables are commonly referred to as "beers," U.S. law requires they be labeled "brews."

Alcohol gives beer body and texture, which is why nonalcoholic versions aren't as satisfying to those used to real beer. On the plus side, besides the minuscule amount of alcohol, there's the reduced calorie count. Whereas an average 12-ounce beer contains around 150 calories (microbrews up to 200), a nonalcoholic brew weighs in somewhere between 60 and 90 calories—just about the midpoint between regular and diet sodas. The calories in beer come primarily from malt, which contains natural sugar in the form of dextrose. But we'll never see a calorie-free brew because malt also contributes a big part of beer's flavor.

The price of nonalcoholic beer is certainly not as light as its flavor—such brews can be costly to produce. Still, they fill a niche and can be eminently more satisfying with a meal than a cloyingly sweet soft drink. Some of the more popular nonalcoholic brews are: Buckler (Heineken),

Cutter (Coors), Haake (Beck), Kaliber (Guinness), Kingsbury, O'Doul's (Anheuser Busch), and St. Pauli Girl.

Nonalcoholic Wines and Beers *see* DEALCOHOLIZED WINES; NONALCOHOLIC BEER

Nutmeg Freshly grated nutmeg has a lively, delicately warm, and spicy flavor. Small jars of whole nutmegs (hard, grayish-brown, egg-shaped seeds about ¾ inch long) can be found in most supermarkets. Several styles of nutmeg graters and grinders are available in kitchenware shops. If you don't have fresh nutmeg, commercially ground nutmeg can be substituted.

Orange-Flower Water A distillation of bitter-orange blossoms with a perfumy orange flavor. Available in supermarkets and liquor stores. *See also* ROSE WATER.

Orgeat Syrup [ohr-ZHAY] An almond-flavored syrup, the original version of which was made from a combination of barley and almonds. Modern-day orgeat syrups are more likely to be a blend of almonds, sugar, and ROSE WATER or ORANGE-FLOWER WATER. Also known as *sirop d'amandes*. Available in liquor stores and some supermarkets. *See also* SYRUPS, FLAVORED.

Quinine Water *see* TONIC WATER

Rose Water A rose-petal distillation with an intensely perfumy flavor and fragrance. Available in liquor stores and many supermarkets. *See also* ORANGE-FLOWER WATER.

Seltzer Water   A flavorless, effervescent water that is more bubbly than many other sparkling waters. Seltzer water has been used in this book instead of CLUB SODA because it has a "cleaner," less salty-citric flavor. Schweppes is the brand most commonly available in supermarkets. The original seltzer water hails from Nieder Selters, a town in Germany's Wiesbaden region. *See also* TONIC WATER; WATER.

Simple Syrup   *see* SUGAR SYRUP

Soda Water   *see* CLUB SODA

Soymilk   A nondairy, iron- and protein-rich liquid produced from pressing ground, cooked soybeans. Soymilk comes in many forms, including regular, sweetened, and flavored. It can be found in supermarkets and natural food stores.

Sugar   Superfine sugar (also called *ultrafine*) is called for in this book for cold drinks because it dissolves so much more quickly than regular granulated sugar. It's commonly available in supermarkets.

Sugar Syrup; Simple Syrup   A combination of sugar and water cooked together (*see recipe,* page 251). For sweetening drinks, use 1½ times the amount of syrup as you would sugar.

Sweetened Condensed Milk   A sticky-sweet mixture of whole milk and sugar, the latter comprising 40 to 45 percent of the whole. Sweetened condensed milk comes in regular and fat-free forms. Unopened cans may be stored at room temperature. After opening, refrigerate and use within 5 days.

Syrups, Flavored   These syrups, made with concentrated fruit juices and other flavorings, can be used to flavor and sweeten myriad drinks. They come in numerous flavors, including almond, apricot, banana, blueberry, caramel, coconut, coffee, cranberry, grenadine, hazelnut, lemon, lime, mango, maple, mint, orange, papaya, passion fruit, raspberry, strawberry, and vanilla. Moderation is the byword when using these syrups, as their flavors are very concentrated. They can be found in liquor stores and some supermarkets. *See also* FALERNUM; GRENADINE; ORGEAT SYRUP; SUGAR SYRUP; and the syrup recipes in the Lagniappe chapter, page 251.

Tofu   This high-protein wonder food is easy to digest, low in calories and sodium, and it's cholesterol-free. It's made from soymilk in a fashion similar to that of making cheese. Tofu comes in whole, low-fat, and nonfat varieties, and in extra-firm, firm, soft, and silken (so named for its silky-smooth texture). Choose soft regular or soft silken tofu for making drinks. Tofu is available in supermarkets and natural food stores. It must be refrigerated and, once opened, should be used within a week (drain off liquid and cover with fresh water).

Tonic Water Effervescent carbon dioxide–charged water flavored with fruit extracts, sugar, and usually a tiny amount of a bitter alkaloid called *quinine*. Tonic water comes in regular and diet forms. It's also sometimes called *quinine water. See also* CLUB SODA; SELTZER WATER.

Triple Sec, Nonalcoholic An alcohol-free version of the well-known orange-flavored original. Rose's Triple Sec is the brand most commonly found—it's available in liquor stores and many supermarkets.

Water Simply put, if water doesn't taste good, neither will anything made with it, from drinks to ice cubes. Bottled distilled or spring water is what you want. *See also* CLUB SODA; SELTZER WATER; TONIC WATER.

Wine *see* DEALCOHOLIZED WINES

Zest The thin, colored portion of a citrus peel.

Ingredient Equivalents

apple   1 medium = 1 scant cup chopped
banana   1 medium = ½ cup puréed
blueberries   1 pint = 2 cups
butter   1 stick = ½ cup; 8 Tbsp.
cantaloupe   1 medium = 3 cups diced
cream   1 cup = 8 oz.; ½ pint; 2 cups whipped
egg   1 large = 3 Tbsp. (yolk = 1 Tbsp.; white = 2 Tbsp.)
egg substitute   ¼ cup = 1 large egg
fruit, canned (most)   15-oz. can = 1⅓ cups drained
fruit, frozen (most)   16-oz. loose pack = 2½ to 3 cups
ginger, fresh   2-inch piece, 1 inch in diameter =
                              2 Tbsp. minced
grapefruit   1 medium = ¾ to 1 cup juice
grapes   1 pound = 2½ to 3 cups
ice cream/sherbet   1 quart = 4 cups
ice cubes   4 to 5 = 1 cup crushed
kiwifruit   2 = ¾ cup chopped
lemon   1 medium = 3 Tbsp. juice plus 2 to 3 tsp. grated peel
lime   1 medium = 1½ Tbsp. juice plus 1 to 1½ tsp. grated peel
marshmallow cream   7- to 7½-oz. jar = 2½ cups
marshmallows, large   1 pound = about 60; 1 cup = 6 to 7
milk, evaporated   5-oz. can = ⅔ cup; 12-oz. can = 1½ cups

milk, sweetened condensed   14-oz. can = 1¾ cups

orange   1 medium = ⅓ cup juice plus 2 Tbsp. grated peel

papaya   1 medium = 1½ to 2 cups chopped

peach   1 medium = ⅔ cup chopped

pear   1 medium = ⅔ cup chopped

pineapple   1 medium = 5 cups cubes

raspberries   ½ pint = 1⅓ cups

strawberries   1 pint = 1½ to 2 cups sliced

sugar, brown   1 pound = 2¼ cups packed

sugar, granulated   1 pound = 2¼ cups

sugar, powdered   1 pound = 4 cups unsifted

sugar, superfine   1 pound = 2⅓ cups

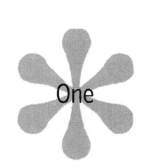

One

Drinks from Around the World

EVERY COUNTRY has its traditional libations, those time-honored drinks that are not only local favorites, but whose popularity has spread far and wide. Countries with hot climates tend toward cool, light drinks, such as Mexico's *aguas frescas* ("fresh waters")—simple, lightly sweetened potions of fruit and water. And India beats the heat with its refreshing *lassis,* which can range from savory renditions flavored with spices like cumin and pepper to sweeter, fruit-flavored versions, my favorite being mango *lassi.* On the flip side of the coin, cold-climate residents need chill-chasers, such as Holland's hot, anise-flavored *anus melk,* and Russia's spicy, honey-based *sbityen.* Then there are holiday favorites, like Puerto Rico's *coquito,* a coconut eggnog. This chapter contains a small sampling of myriad drinks from around the world, some of which may just become favorites in your household.

See also Affogatto, page 153; Arabic Coffee, page 148; Café de Olla, page 144; Café Shakerato, page 155 Chai Tea, page 161; Glögg, page 215; Glühwein, page 192; Greek Coffee, page 148; Lamoonada, page 78; Mexican Hot Chocolate, page 188; Mexican Mocha, page 144; Sangría, page 226; Thai Iced Tea, page 177; Turkish Coffee, page 147; Viennese Coffee, page 146.

Agua de Jamaica
[AH-gwah day hah-MY-kah] (Mexico)

Agua fresca [AH-gwah FRES-kah], "fresh water," is the Spanish term for a refreshing beverage made with water, sugar, and fruit (rind or flesh) or flowers. This rendition uses dried Jamaica flowers (*see* page 29), which produce a sour-sweet flavor and shimmering crimson color.

SERVES 4

⅔ cup loose Jamaica flowers

5 cups (40 oz.) water

½ to 1 cup sugar

In a medium, nonreactive saucepan, combine flowers and 1½ cups of the water. Bring to a boil over medium heat; cook for 5 minutes. Remove from heat; add sugar, stirring to dissolve. Stir in remaining 3½ cups water. Cover and refrigerate overnight. Strain and serve in tall, ice-filled glasses.

Atole [ah-TOH-leh] (Mexico)

Popular in Mexico and parts of the American Southwest, this beverage is said to date back to pre-Columbian times. It's thickened with *masa harina* (lime-treated, dried corn kernels ground into flour). Masa harina and Mexican chocolate can be found in Latin markets and many supermarkets. Latin markets sell instant atole, which can be mixed with milk or water. Atole can be served hot or at room temperature. Following are a few of the many atole renditions. See also Tips for Making Hot Drinks, page 184.

Atole de Chocolate (also called Champurrado)

SERVES 4

2 cups (16 oz.) chilled water
rounded ⅓ cup masa harina
½ cinnamon stick
2 cups (16 oz.) whole milk

3 oz. Mexican chocolate or bittersweet chocolate, chopped

⅓ cup packed dark brown sugar

1 tsp. pure vanilla extract

In a medium bowl, gradually stir 1 cup of the water into masa harina. Let stand 15 minutes. In a medium, heavy saucepan, bring remaining 1 cup water and cinnamon stick to a boil. Pour masa harina mixture through a fine sieve into boiling water, stirring constantly. Add milk, chocolate, and sugar; stir over medium-low heat until chocolate melts and mixture is creamy and smooth. Remove from heat; stir in vanilla. Whisk lightly until atole is frothy. Serve immediately in warm mugs, or cool to room temperature, refrigerate, and serve cold in medium glasses. Use a whisk to froth the mixture before serving.

Plain Atole

SERVES 4

2 cups (16 oz.) chilled water

rounded ⅓ cup masa harina

2 cups (16 oz.) whole milk

¼ cup packed dark brown sugar

¼ tsp. ground cinnamon

1 tsp. pure vanilla extract

In a medium bowl, gradually stir 1 cup of the water into masa harina. Let stand 15 minutes. In a medium, heavy saucepan, bring remaining 1 cup water to a boil. Pour masa harina mixture through a fine sieve into boiling water, stirring constantly. Add milk, sugar, and cinnamon; stir over medium-low heat until mixture is creamy and smooth. Remove from heat; stir in vanilla. Whisk lightly until atole is frothy. Serve hot.

VARIATIONS

Atole de Piña [ah-TOH-leh day PEE-nyah] (pineapple) Before beginning recipe, pour an undrained 20-oz. can crushed pineapple in juice into a blender. Process at medium-high until puréed; set aside until ready to use. Substitute pineapple purée for the milk.

Atole de Bayas [ah-TOH-leh day BAH-yahs] (berries) Before beginning recipe, purée 3 cups hulled strawberries in a blender at medium-high speed. Strain through a fine sieve, if desired; set aside until ready to use. Substitute strawberry purée for the milk; omit cinnamon.

Horchata [hor-CHAH-tah] (Mexico; Spain)

There are myriad variations of these light, thirst-quenching coolers, all made by steeping in water any of various ingredients, such as nuts, grains (rice being the most common), seeds (such as sesame), or *chufa,* a tuber that can be found in its dried form in Latin markets. Horchatas are typically served cold or at room temperature. Following are three versions.

Horchata de Almendras

[hor-CHAH-tah day ahl-MEHN (MAYN)-drahs] (almonds)

SERVES 8

1 cup blanched almonds, coarsely ground
coarsely grated zest of ½ medium lemon, or
   1 whole lime
8 cups (64 oz.) water
about 1 cup superfine sugar

In a medium bowl, combine almonds, citrus zest, and 3 cups hot water. Cover and let stand at least 6 hours at room temperature. Transfer mixture to a blender; process at medium speed for 1 minute. Add 2 cups water; blend 20 seconds more at medium speed. Line a medium-large, fine sieve with a triple layer of fine cheesecloth that has been dampened and wrung out. Set cloth-lined sieve over a large pitcher or bowl. Pour mixture through sieve in 3 batches, stirring and pressing to push the liquid through the solids. After all the liquid has passed through, gather the corners of the cloth and twist to extract as much liquid as possible; discard cloth. Add sugar to taste and remaining 3 cups water, stirring to dissolve sugar. Cover and refrigerate until very cold, at least 3 hours. Serve in medium, ice-filled glasses.

VARIATIONS

Horchata de Arroz [ah-RROHS] (rice)   Substitute 1 cup white rice that has been pulverized in the blender for the almonds, omit citrus zest, and add 1 cinnamon stick. Remove cinnamon stick before blending.

Horchata de Ajonjolí [ah-hohn-hoh-LEE] (sesame) Substitute 2 cups toasted sesame seeds for the almonds (toast seeds in a dry skillet over high heat, stirring often, until golden brown).

 For centuries the pineapple (in the form of carved wood, stone sculptures, and so on) has been used as a symbol of hospitality.

Bebida de Piña
[beh-BEE-dah day PEE-nyah] (Spain; Mexico)

Bebida is Spanish for "drink," *piña* for "pineapple."

SERVES 1

¾ cup drained crushed pineapple packed in juice

½ cup (4 oz.) fresh orange juice

¼ tsp. pure vanilla extract

4 ice cubes, coarsely crushed
mint sprig for garnish

Combine all ingredients except garnish in a blender. Cover and process at high speed until smooth. Pour into a tall glass; garnish with mint sprig.

Anus Melk (Holland)

This warmer is known as "anise milk" in the Netherlands. Toasting the anise seed will intensify the flavor.

SERVES 4

1 rounded Tbsp. anise seed, crushed
4 cups (32 oz.) milk
½ cup sugar
2 Tbsp. (1 oz.) cornstarch
2 Tbsp. (1 oz.) water

Combine anise seed, milk, and sugar in a medium saucepan. Cook over medium heat until mixture begins to simmer. Reduce heat to low; cook 5 minutes. Meanwhile, place cornstarch in a small bowl. Gradually add water, stirring until smooth. Stirring constantly, slowly add cornstarch mixture to milk. Simmer, stirring constantly, for 5 minutes. Pour through a fine strainer into warmed mugs. May be served immediately, or cooled to room temperature, refrigerated, and reheated over medium-low heat (don't let it boil) just before serving.

Ayran [EYE-ran] (Turkey)

This refreshing, nonsweetened yogurt drink is popular throughout the Middle East. Ayran is called *abdug* in Iran and *than* in Armenia.

SERVES 4

2 cups (16 oz.) plain low-fat yogurt
2 cups (16 oz.) ice water
salt

Combine yogurt and water in a blender. Cover and process at medium speed until smooth. Salt to taste. Cover and chill well before serving. Serve in tall, ice-filled glasses.

VARIATIONS

Garlic Ayran   Add 1 small garlic clove, minced (or a pinch of garlic powder), before blending.

Mint Ayran   Add 1 to 2 tsp. minced fresh mint before blending; garnish each serving with mint sprig.

Ayran Fizz   Fill tall, ice-filled glasses two-thirds full with ayran. Top with chilled seltzer water or club soda; stir gently.

Boisson à la Grenade

[bwah-SAWN ah lah greh-NAHD] (North Africa)

This is a perfect quencher for hot summer days. *Grenade* is French for "pomegranate," from which the original grenadine was made.

SERVES 4

3 cups (24 oz.) chilled water
½ cup (4 oz.) grenadine
½ cup (4 oz.) lemon juice
1 tsp. orange-flower water
superfine sugar

In a large pitcher, stir together water, grenadine, lemon juice, and orange-flower water. Add sugar to taste, stirring to dissolve. Pour into tall, ice-filled glasses.

VARIATION

Grenade Fizz   Combine all ingredients except water in a pitcher; mix well. Substitute chilled seltzer water or club soda for the water, slowly pouring into pitcher; stir gently.

Coquito [koh-KEE-toh] (Puerto Rico)

Coconut eggnog is a Puerto Rican Christmas tradition and can be prepared both with and without the addition of rum. Coconut milk is available in regular and low-fat versions in most supermarkets.

SERVES 8

2 14-oz. cans low-fat coconut milk
1 12-oz. can sweetened condensed milk
4 egg yolks or ⅓ cup egg substitute
2 tsp. pure vanilla extract

½ tsp. ground cinnamon
2 cups (16 oz.) whole milk

Combine all ingredients except whole milk in a blender. Cover and process at medium-low speed until smooth. Add whole milk; blend at low speed until combined. Cover and chill until very cold, at least 3 hours. Stir well before serving in small glasses without ice; dust servings with additional ground cinnamon, if desired.

Lassi [LAH-see] (India)

India's lassis (yogurt-based smoothies) are not only immensely popular but also thirst-quenching and nutritious. There are three basic styles of lassi—sweet, salty (savory), and fruit-based. To approximate the extra-rich yogurt found in India, use a combination of whole-milk yogurt and sour cream. Calorie watchers can substitute all low- or nonfat yogurt, but the end result won't taste as authentic or rich.

Plain Sweet Lassi

SERVES 4

3 cups (24 oz.) plain or vanilla whole-milk yogurt
(or 2½ cups yogurt plus ½ cup sour cream)
½ cup (4 oz.) ice water
½ cup superfine sugar

¼ tsp. salt

8 ice cubes, coarsely crushed

Combine all ingredients in a blender. Cover and process at medium-high speed until smooth. Pour into medium glasses; sprinkle lightly with more sugar, if desired.

Savory Lassi

SERVES 4

3 cups (24 oz.) plain or lemon whole-milk yogurt
(or 2½ cups yogurt plus ½ cup sour cream)

⅓ cup (scant 3 oz.) ice water

2 Tbsp. (1 oz.) fresh lemon or lime juice

1 tsp. ground cumin

½ tsp. salt

½ tsp. freshly ground pepper (optional)

8 ice cubes, coarsely crushed

Combine all ingredients in a blender. Cover and process at medium-high speed until smooth. Pour into medium glasses; sprinkle lightly with additional cumin.

Mint Lassi

SERVES 4

⅓ cup loosely packed mint leaves

3 cups (24 oz.) plain or vanilla whole-milk yogurt
(or 2½ cups yogurt plus ½ cup sour cream)

⅓ cup (scant 3 oz.) ice water

½ cup superfine sugar

1½ tsp. rose water

8 ice cubes, coarsely crushed

4 mint sprigs for garnish

Combine all ingredients except garnish in a blender. Cover and process at medium-high speed until smooth. Pour into medium glasses; garnish with mint sprigs.

VARIATION

Coriander Lassi   Substitute fresh coriander (cilantro) leaves for the mint. Garnish with sprigs of coriander.

Mango Lassi

Although rich milk is traditional for mango lassi, buttermilk or yogurt may be substituted with equally delicious results. If mangoes aren't in season, use mango pulp, available in Indian and Latin markets. For the best results, place both mango and milk in the freezer for 20 minutes before starting this recipe. And for a *completely nontraditional* but absolutely delicious rendition, try the Tropical Fruit Lassi variation.

SERVES 4

1 large mango, peeled and chopped, or 1 cup
    mango pulp

2½ cups (20 oz.) icy-cold rich milk, buttermilk, or
    yogurt
¼ cup superfine sugar or honey
4 mango slices for garnish (optional)

Combine all ingredients except garnish in a blender. Cover
and process at medium-high speed until smooth. Pour into
medium glasses; garnish with mango slices, if desired.

VARIATION

Tropical Fruit Lassi   Substitute low-fat coconut milk
for the milk, and use any tropical fruit such as mango,
papaya, or guava.   .

Sbityen [ZBEET-yen] (Russia)

Although this honey-based warmer usually contains a jolt
of vodka or brandy, it's equally wonderful without it. *See
also* Tips for Making Hot Drinks, page 184.

SERVES 6

6 cups (48 oz.) water
⅔ cup (scant 6 oz.) honey
2-inch piece (½ inch in diameter) peeled ginger,
    thinly sliced
grated zest of 1 small lemon
1 stick cinnamon, broken in half

10 whole cloves

5 peppercorns

½ bay leaf

ground cinnamon for garnish (optional)

Combine all ingredients except garnish in a medium saucepan. Bring to a boil, stirring occasionally to dissolve honey. Reduce heat to low; cover and simmer 20 minutes. Strain into mugs; sprinkle with cinnamon, if desired. May be refrigerated and reheated.

Shandy (Britain)

Short for *shandygaff*, this British drink originated in the middle of the nineteenth century. Use a full-flavored beer, such as O'Doul's Amber.

SERVES 2

1 12-oz. bottle chilled nonalcoholic beer

1 12-oz. bottle chilled nonalcoholic ginger beer, ginger ale, or lemonade

One hour before serving, place 2 glass mugs or tall glasses in the freezer to become frosty. Pour half the beer and half the ginger beer, ginger ale, or lemonade into each mug or glass.

✳ **The smell of almonds toasting in a metal pan is the most agreeable incense I know. . . . I am decidedly addicted to their perfume.**

—Bert Greene, American author, journalist, playwright

Sharbat Bil Looz (Morocco)

This almond-milk drink is mildly sweet and exceedingly satisfying. Although classically served chilled, it's immensely soothing when warm. Although not traditional, toasting the almonds adds a rich flavor. For even more almond flavor, add a drop of pure almond extract.

SERVES 4

1½ cups (12 oz.) water

8 oz. slivered almonds, toasted, if desired

½ cup superfine sugar

1½ cups (12 oz.) milk

1 to 2 dashes (¹⁄₁₆ to ⅛ tsp.) orange-flower water
   or rose water

1 drop pure almond extract (optional)

Combine 1 cup of the water, almonds, and sugar in a blender. Cover and process at medium speed until smooth. Add remaining ½ cup water, milk, and orange-

flower water; process until combined. Pour through a
fine strainer into a pitcher. Taste and add almond
extract, if desired. Cover and chill at least 1 hour. Pour
into small glasses.

Yansoon (Arab countries)

This spicy, warming drink is extremely popular throughout Arab countries. Although it is not traditional to do so,
yansoon is also wonderful made with milk. *See also* Tips
for Making Hot Drinks, page 184.

SERVES 4

4 cups (32 oz.) water
1-inch piece (½ inch in diameter) peeled ginger,
    thinly sliced
6 whole star anise
5 whole cloves
1 cinnamon stick
sugar
2 Tbsp. toasted sliced almonds for
    garnish
4 cinnamon sticks for garnish (optional)

Combine water, ginger, anise, cloves, and cinnamon stick
in a large saucepan. Bring to a boil; cook 5 minutes.
Sweeten to taste with sugar. Strain yansoon into warm

mugs. Sprinkle each serving with almonds; garnish with cinnamon stick, if desired.

VARIATION

Yansoon Milk Substitute milk for the water. Bring ingredients to a simmer over low heat; cook for 5 minutes.

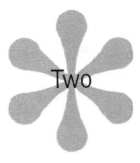

Two

Coolers

Sparkling Quenchers: Spritzers,
Juleps, Tonics, and Rickeys

A CLASSIC COOLER is a tall, iced drink of wine or liquor mixed with a carbonated beverage. I've broadened the category to include a bevy of sparkling libations—sans alcohol, of course, but full of thirst-quenching refreshment. The thing to remember about carbonated beverages, from seltzer water to cola, is to keep them refrigerated. Chilled sparklers seem to produce more sparkle than those poured at room temperature. The bonus, of course, is that cold ingredients won't melt ice cubes and dilute drinks as fast as room-temperature mixtures. Speaking of ice cubes, be sure to check out Flavored Ice Cubes, page 261—they'll add flavor and pizzazz to your coolers.

Egg Cream

This famous New York concoction contains neither eggs *nor* cream, but that doesn't deter its fans. There are a few secrets to making the quintessential egg cream: Use a rich, dark chocolate syrup—purists demand Fox's U-Bet chocolate syrup (available through www.foodlocker.com); all ingredients must be chilled; don't even think about using anything but whole milk; if possible, use seltzer water from a siphon bottle—it's livelier and has more bubbles than bottled seltzer. Lastly, tradition says that one always drinks an egg cream standing up.

SERVES 1

½ cup (4 oz.) chilled whole milk
about ¾ cup (6 oz.) chilled seltzer water
2 to 3 Tbsp. (1 to 1½ oz.) chilled Fox's U-Bet chocolate
    syrup or Dark Chocolate Syrup, page 256

Pour milk into a tall glass. Squirt seltzer into glass, filling just until mixture forms a rounded, foamy head at rim of glass. Or pour bottled seltzer into glass, stirring vigorously until foam rises to glass rim. Drizzle chocolate syrup into glass. Use an iced-tea spoon to stir milk and chocolate together without disturbing the foamy head. Serve immediately.

Ginger Julep

The word "julep" comes from the Persian *julâb*, meaning "rose water." In fifteenth-century England the word evolved to describe a flavored sugar syrup, often added to medication. Today, it's used to describe mint julep (*see* Mint Julep Tea, page 172) as well as other sweet, light drinks served over crushed ice.

SERVES 1

8 large, fresh mint leaves
1 tsp. superfine sugar
1 tsp. water
1 tsp. grenadine
about 1 cup crushed ice
about ¾ cup (6 oz.) chilled ginger ale
large mint sprig for garnish

Muddle mint leaves, sugar, water, and grenadine in a julep cup or tall glass until leaves are crushed and sugar is dissolved. Fill the cup or glass with crushed ice. Top with ginger ale, stirring gently but well. Add more crushed ice, if necessary, so beverage comes to within ½ inch of glass rim. Garnish with mint sprig; serve with a straw.

✳ **When one has tasted watermelons one knows what angels eat. It was not a Southern watermelon that Eve took; we know it because she repented.**

—Mark Twain, American author, humorist

Watermelon Whirl

Watermelon drinks can sometimes be a little grainy. If you don't mind the texture, don't bother straining the mixture.

SERVES 4

3 cups seeded, chopped watermelon
1 cup (8 oz.) ice water
2 Tbsp. (1 oz.) fresh lime juice
¼ cup superfine sugar
¼ tsp. ground allspice
12 watermelon ice cubes, page 261 (optional)
4 mint sprigs for garnish

Combine all ingredients except ice and garnish in a blender. Cover and process at high speed until smooth. Pour through a fine strainer, dividing evenly between 4 tall glasses; add ice cubes, if desired. Garnish with mint sprigs.

VARIATIONS

Watermelon-Mint Whirl   Add 8 large mint leaves before blending.

Watermelon Spritz   Divide watermelon
mixture evenly between 4 tall glasses. Add 3
watermelon ice cubes to each glass. Top with chilled
sparkling water or ginger ale, stirring gently to
combine.

Limey Cooler

Both the juice and the zest of limes are used in this
sparkler. Be sure to remove only the skin's zest (green portion), as the white pith is bitter.

SERVES 5 TO 6

8 large limes
½ tsp. salt
1 to 1½ cups sugar
2 cups (16 oz.) very hot water
4 cups (32 oz.) chilled sparkling water

Working with a fine grater over a medium bowl, remove
zest from limes. Add salt and 1 cup of the sugar to zest;
muddle for about 30 seconds. Add hot water, stirring to
dissolve sugar. Set aside 1 hour to steep. Meanwhile,
squeeze juice from 4 of the limes and pour into a large
pitcher (wrap and reserve remaining limes for another
use). Place a fine sieve lined with a double layer of
cheesecloth over pitcher; strain lime-zest mixture
through it, pressing to extract as much liquid as

possible. Cover and chill. Sweeten with additional sugar, if desired. Just before serving, pour in sparkling water. Serve in tall, ice-filled glasses.

VARIATION

Ginger-Limey Cooler   Add 1 Tbsp. grated ginger to lime zest before muddling and steeping. Substitute chilled ginger ale for chilled sparkling water.

Jamaican Cola

This drink gets its name from three of Jamaica's primary crops—coffee, cocoa, and allspice.

SERVES 1

1 tsp. instant espresso powder
2 tsp. hot water
¼ cup (2 oz.) half & half
1½ Tbsp. (¾ oz.) Dark Chocolate Syrup, page 256, or store-bought chocolate syrup
pinch of ground allspice
¾ to 1 cup (6 to 8 oz.) chilled cola

In a tall glass, dissolve espresso powder in hot water. Add half & half, chocolate syrup, and allspice; stir to combine. Add 3 to 5 ice cubes. Top with cola, stirring to combine.

Passionflower

You'll find passion fruit nectar in supermarkets and grenadine in liquor stores.

SERVES 1

⅜ cup (3 oz.) passion fruit nectar
1 Tbsp. (½ oz.) grenadine
1 Tbsp. (½ oz.) fresh lime juice
about ½ cup (4 oz.) chilled ginger ale
lime slice for garnish

Pour the first 3 ingredients into a tall glass and stir well. Add 3 to 4 ice cubes; top with ginger ale, stirring gently. Garnish with lime slice.

Passion Perfect

SORRY, CUPIDS, the tropically grown passion fruit is not named for the passion it produces, however one might wish it. The name actually comes from the spectacularly showy passionflower of the same plant. When Spanish conquistadores discovered this exotic flower, they saw the various parts as symbolic of the passion of Christ's crucifixion—the fringelike crown, likened to the crown of thorns, tendrils resembling whips, and so on. And therein lies a name.

Ginger Jazz

A refreshing spritzer that's also good for upset tummies.

SERVES 1

½-inch piece (½ inch in diameter) peeled ginger
2 Tbsp. (1 oz.) Ginger Syrup, page 252, or store-
    bought ginger-flavored syrup
about ¾ cup (6 oz.) chilled ginger ale
mint sprig for garnish

Smash ginger with a mallet or other heavy utensil; drop into a tall glass. Add ginger syrup; fill glass with ice cubes. Top with ginger ale, stirring well. Garnish with mint.

VARIATION

Hot Ginger Jazz Place ginger and ginger syrup in a warm mug. Fill with boiling water; stir to combine. Sprinkle with ground ginger, if desired. *See also* Tips for Making Hot Drinks, page 184.

Caramel Apple Kiss

SERVES 1

2 Tbsp. (1 oz.) Ooey-Gooey Caramel Sauce, page
    257, or store-bought caramel sauce
⅔ cup (scant 6 oz.) apple juice

about ½ cup (4 oz.) chilled seltzer water or club
soda
apple slice for garnish

Pour caramel sauce and apple juice into a tall glass; stir
well. Add 3 to 4 ice cubes; top with seltzer. Garnish with
apple slice.

Lime Rickey

The drink-related use of the word "rickey" was coined in the
late 1800s in Washington, D.C., purportedly after the name of
congressional lobbyist and renowned tippler Joe Rickey.

SERVES 1

¼ cup (2 oz.) Zesty Lime Syrup, page 254, or
store-bought lime-flavored syrup
1 Tbsp. (½ oz.) fresh lime juice
about 1 cup (8 oz.) chilled seltzer water
lime wedge for garnish
maraschino cherry (optional)

Pour the first 2 ingredients into a tall, ice-filled glass.
Top with seltzer, stirring gently. Garnish with lime
wedge and cherry, if desired.

VARIATION

Ginger-Lime Rickey   Substitute ginger ale for the
seltzer; add chunk of candied ginger.

Golden Glow

SERVES 1

¼ cup (2 oz.) apricot nectar
¼ cup (2 oz.) apple juice
¼ cup (2 oz.) fresh orange juice
2 tsp. fresh lime juice
about ½ cup (4 oz.) chilled tonic water
1 tsp. grenadine
orange wedge for garnish

In a tall glass, stir together the first 4 ingredients; add 3 to 5 ice cubes. Top with tonic water, stirring gently. Add grenadine; don't stir. Garnish with orange wedge.

 I'll be with you in the squeezing of a lemon.
—Oliver Goldsmith, British author, playwright

Blushing Lemon Squash

In Britain, the word "squash" is used for a citrus-based soft drink. Add Sugar Syrup (page 251) or superfine sugar for a sweeter drink.

SERVES 1

2 Tbsp. (1 oz.) lemon juice
1 Tbsp. (½ oz.) grenadine

about ¾ cup (6 oz.) chilled seltzer water or club soda
lemon slice for garnish

Combine lemon juice and grenadine in a tall glass; add 3 to 4 ice cubes. Top with seltzer; stir gently. Garnish with lemon slice.

Beach Breeze

Add an exotic touch by substituting cranberry-mango or cranberry-tangerine juice for the cranberry juice.

SERVES 1

½ cup (4 oz.) unsweetened pineapple juice
¼ cup (2 oz.) cranberry juice
about ½ cup (4 oz.) chilled lime-flavored sparkling water
mint sprig for garnish

Pour juices into a tall, ice-filled glass. Top with sparkling water, stirring gently. Garnish with mint sprig.

Orange Rush

For extra-orangy flavor, use ⅓ cup frozen orange juice concentrate and ⅔ cup chilled water instead of the fresh orange juice

SERVES 1

1 cup (8 oz.) chilled fresh orange juice
2 tsp. grenadine

about ½ cup (4 oz.) chilled orange-flavored
sparkling water
orange slice for garnish

In a tall glass, mix orange juice and grenadine. Add 3 to 4 ice cubes; top with sparkling water, stirring gently. Garnish with orange slice.

 While forbidden fruit is said to taste sweeter, it usually spoils faster.

—Abigail Van Buren, American columnist, author

Love Potion

Mark Twain once said: "India has 2,000,000 gods, and worships them all. In religion other countries are paupers; India is the only millionaire." Coconut, considered a gift from the gods in India, is said to bring romantic good fortune. Try this exotic potion and see for yourself.

SERVES 1

¾ cup (6 oz.) low-fat coconut milk
¼ tsp. rose water

1 Tbsp. (½ oz.) Sugar Syrup, page 251 (optional)
chilled seltzer water

In a tall glass, combine coconut milk, rose water, and
sugar syrup, if desired. Add 3 to 5 ice cubes; top with
seltzer water, stirring gently.

Purple Passion

SERVES 1

⅜ cup (3 oz.) chilled purple grape juice
⅜ cup (3 oz.) chilled unsweetened grapefruit juice
¼ cup (2 oz.) chilled ginger ale

Stir juices together in a tall glass. Add 3 to 4 ice cubes;
gradually stir in ginger ale.

Apple-Lime Cooler

SERVES 1

about 1 cup crushed ice
¾ cup (6 oz.) apple juice
1 Tbsp. (½ oz.) fresh lime juice
about ½ cup (4 oz.) lime-flavored sparkling water
lime slice for garnish

In a tall glass filled with crushed ice, stir
together apple and lime juices. Top with sparkling
water; garnish with lime slice.

Spritzer

For this refreshing drink, use your favorite flavored syrup and seltzer water—what could be easier? Supermarkets and liquor stores carry myriad syrups, ranging in flavor from blueberry to hazelnut to peppermint. Of course, you can always make your own syrup (*see* the Lagniappe chapter, page 251) to suit your personal taste.

SERVES 1

> 2 to 3 Tbsp. (1 to 1½ oz.) flavored syrup, store-bought or homemade (*see* pages 251–256)
> 1 cup (8 oz.) seltzer or other sparkling water

Fill a tall glass with ice cubes. Add syrup and seltzer, stirring to combine.

VARIATION

Wine Spritzer   Pour ½ cup (4 oz.) dealcoholized red or white wine into a wineglass. Add 2 to 3 ice cubes. Top with seltzer and stir gently.

Three

First Ades

Lemonades, Limeades, and
All Kinds of Other Ades

ALTHOUGH AMERICANS
consider lemonade as
quintessentially theirs,
history tells us that this
lively libation was invented
in Paris in 1630 when imported sugar
became more affordable. *Citron pressé*
(lemonade) is served in France in its purest
form—a glass containing a small amount of
fresh, pulpy lemon juice, accompanied by a
carafe of water and a bowl of superfine
sugar or a small pitcher of sugar syrup.
Individuals can sweeten and dilute the juice
to personalize the drink to their taste.

The term "ade" is broad, however, and doesn't necessarily refer to lemon-based beverages. In truth, any combination of citrus juice, sweetener, and water can be called "ade." I've even stepped outside the box in this chapter to create Carrotade, page 78. You can enliven any ade by floating thin slices of lemon, lime, orange, or whatever fruit the drink's based on.

Old-Fashioned Lemonade

Tried and true and simple enough to be child's play.

SERVES 6

1 cup (8 oz.) fresh lemon juice
1 cup superfine sugar
4 cups (32 oz.) water
1 whole lemon, cut into ¼-inch slices for garnish
(optional)

Combine all ingredients except garnish in a large pitcher; stir to dissolve sugar. Add lemon slices, if desired. Serve in tall, ice-filled glasses.

VARIATIONS

Lemonade Crush Reduce water to 3 cups (24 oz.). Pour lemonade into tall glasses filled with crushed ice.

Lavender Lemonade At least 1 hour ahead of time, combine 1 cup (8 oz.) boiling water with 2 Tbsp. dried or ¼ cup fresh lavender leaves. Cover and let steep 1 hour.

Strain lavender water into pitcher; proceed with recipe, adding only 3 cups (24 oz.) water.

✳ When life gives you lemons, make lemonade!

Instant Lemonade Mix

Keep this in the fridge for an instant glass of lemonade whenever the mood strikes.

SERVES 12

2 cups (16 oz.) fresh lemon juice
1 cup (8 oz.) light corn syrup
¾ cup superfine sugar

In a 1-quart container, mix all ingredients, stirring until sugar dissolves. Cover and refrigerate for up to 2 weeks. For each serving, stir well and pour ¼ cup (2 oz.) into a tall glass. Add ¾ cup (6 oz.) chilled water (still or sparkling), stirring to combine; add ice cubes.

VARIATIONS

Instant Pink Lemonade Mix   Substitute grenadine for the corn syrup.

Instant Limeade Mix   Substitute fresh lime juice for the lemon juice; add a few drops of green food coloring, if desired.

Zesty Lemonade

Lemon zest adds pizzazz to this lemonade, which can be made either in individual servings or for a group.

SERVES 12 TO 14

1 recipe Zesty Lemon Syrup, page 253
10 cups (80 oz.) chilled water
lemon slices or mint sprigs for garnish
   (optional)

Pour lemon syrup and water into a large pitcher, stirring to combine. Cover and chill until ready to serve. Pour into tall, ice-filled glasses; garnish with lemon slices or mint sprigs, if desired.

VARIATIONS

Sparkling Lemonade   Substitute chilled sparkling water for the water.

Lemonade Tonic   Substitute chilled tonic water for the water.

Individual Lemonade   In a tall glass, stir together ¼ cup (2 oz.) lemon syrup and ¾ cup (6 oz.) water; add ice cubes.

Zesty Limeade   Substitute Zesty Lime Syrup, page 254, for the lemon syrup; use only 8 cups (64 oz.) water. A few drops of green food coloring may be added, if desired.

Lemon Logic

W HEN YOU need both zest and juice of a
lemon or other citrus fruit, remove the zest
first, then cut the fruit in half and squeeze out the
juice. For maximum juice, roll the fruit a couple of
times firmly between your palm and the countertop. Or prick the skin in several places (without
penetrating the flesh) and microwave the fruit at
HIGH for 10 to 20 seconds; let it stand for 1 minute
before rolling it on the countertop and squeezing.

Orangeade

Using Zesty Orange Syrup for the sweetener makes this
orangeade something special.

SERVES 10

6 cups (48 oz.) fresh orange juice

⅔ cup (scant 6 oz.) Zesty Orange Syrup, page 253,
or ½ cup superfine sugar

4 cups (32 oz.) chilled seltzer or other sparkling
water

1 orange, cut into ¼-inch slices for garnish

In a large pitcher, combine orange juice and orange
syrup or sugar, stirring to combine. Add seltzer, stirring
gently; add orange slices. Pour into tall, ice-filled glasses.

VARIATION

Honeyed Orangeade Substitute honey for the orange syrup.

✳ **... there is nothing more delicious than an orange. The very sound of the word, the dazzling exotic color that shimmers inside the word, is a poem of surpassing beauty, complete in this line:**
Orange
—Joyce Carol Oates, American writer

Bubbleade

This couldn't be more refreshing or easier to make. And it has as many variations as you have imagination. One of my favorite combos is Hawaii's Own brand guava-passion-orange frozen juice concentrate mixed with lime-flavored sparkling water. Some frozen concentrates don't come in 12-ounce sizes, in which case simply use two 6-ounce cans.

SERVES 6

1 12-oz. can (or 2 6-oz. cans) frozen juice
   concentrate, thawed

4½ cups (36 oz.) chilled sparkling water (flavored
or plain) or ginger ale
fruit slices for garnish (optional)

Turn juice concentrate into a serving pitcher. Add about
1 cup of the sparkling water, stirring to mix well. Slowly
add remaining sparkling water, stirring gently. Pour into
tall, ice-filled glasses. If desired, garnish with a slice of
the same fruit as the flavor of the concentrate.

Banana Lemonade

A nice change of pace and a great way to use soft bananas.

SERVES 1

1 medium ripe banana, peeled and quartered
¼ cup (2 oz.) fresh lemon juice
⅓ cup (scant 3 oz.) chilled water
3 to 4 Tbsp. superfine sugar
3 ice cubes, coarsely crushed
lemon slice for garnish

Combine all ingredients except garnish in a blender.
Cover and process at high speed until smooth. Pour into
a tall glass; add ice cubes. Garnish with lemon slice.

VARIATION

Banana Limeade   Substitute fresh lime juice for the
lemon juice; garnish with lime slice.

Carrotade

Easy, refreshing, and oh, so good for you!

SERVES 1

⅔ cup (scant 6 oz.) carrot juice
1 Tbsp. (½ oz.) fresh lemon or lime juice
superfine sugar or Sugar Syrup, page 251
  (optional)
about ⅔ cup (scant 6 oz.) chilled lemon-lime soda
lemon or lime slice for garnish

Combine carrot juice, lemon or lime juice, and sweetener, if desired, to taste in a tall glass. Add 3 to 4 ice cubes; top with soda, stirring gently. Garnish with lemon or lime slice.

Lamoonada

Orange-flower water gives this refreshing Middle Eastern lemonade an exotic touch. The sparkling water isn't traditional, but gives the cooler a lively sparkle.

SERVES 1

1 medium lemon, cut in half
3 drops orange-flower water
1 to 3 Tbsp. superfine sugar
chilled still or sparkling water

Squeeze lemon juice into a tall glass. Add orange-flower water and sugar to taste, stirring to dissolve sugar. Add 3 to 4 ice cubes; fill with water, stirring to combine.

Sunburst Limonade

SERVES 10

2 cups (16 oz.) fresh orange juice
1 cup (8 oz.) fresh lime juice
½ cup (4 oz.) fresh lemon juice
8 cups (64 oz.) chilled water
1 to 1½ cups superfine sugar
1 *each* orange, lemon, and lime, cut into ¼-inch slices for garnish

Combine all ingredients except garnish in a large pitcher, stirring until sugar dissolves. Add orange, lemon, and lime slices. Cover and refrigerate until ready to serve. Serve in tall, ice-filled glasses.

✳ **Eat ginger and you will love and be loved as in your youth.**
—Italian saying

Sparkling Gingerade

This refresher can be made 3 days in advance, and the recipe doubles easily.

SERVES 6

3 cups (24 oz.) water

4-inch piece (1 inch in diameter) peeled ginger, thinly sliced

zest of 2 large lemons

⅔ cup sugar

⅓ cup (scant 3 oz.) honey

6 large mint leaves

6 whole cloves

1 cup (8 oz.) fresh lemon juice

about 3 cups (24 oz.) chilled ginger ale

6 mint sprigs for garnish

In a medium saucepan, combine water, ginger, lemon zest, sugar, honey, mint leaves, and cloves; bring to a boil. Reduce heat; cover and simmer for 10 minutes. Remove from heat; cool to room temperature. Strain into a pitcher; stir in lemon juice. Cover and refrigerate until chilled, about 3 hours. To serve, place 3 to 4 ice cubes in tall glasses. Fill halfway with Gingerade; top with ginger ale, stirring gently. Garnish with mint sprigs.

Strawberry Lemonade

SERVES 10

6 cups (48 oz.) chilled water

1 16-oz. package frozen whole strawberries, partially thawed

1 12-oz. can frozen pink lemonade
   concentrate
whole fresh strawberries for garnish (optional)

Combine 3 cups of the water, half the packaged strawberries, and half the lemonade concentrate in a blender. Cover and process at high speed until smooth; pour into a pitcher. Repeat with the remaining water, strawberries, and concentrate. Add to pitcher, stirring well. Pour into tall, ice-filled glasses. Garnish with whole strawberries, if desired. Serve with straws and iced-tea spoons.

Limelight

SERVES 4

1 cup (8 oz.) Zesty Lime Syrup, page 254
3 cups (24 oz.) chilled lime-flavored sparkling
   water
lime slices for garnish

Pour ¼ cup lime syrup into each of 4 tall glasses; add 4 to 5 ice cubes. Top with sparkling water, stirring gently. Garnish with lime slices.

VARIATION

Ginger Limelight   Substitute chilled ginger ale for the sparkling water.

Hot Honey Lemonade

Whether you have a cold, or are weary, or maybe just plain grumpy, this old-fashioned soother is the perfect pick-me-up. *See also* Tips for Making Hot Drinks, page 184.

SERVES 1

¾ to 1 cup (6 to 8 oz.) boiling water
2 Tbsp. (1 oz.) honey
1 Tbsp. (½ oz.) fresh lemon juice
pinch of ground cinnamon
pinch of ground ginger

Combine all ingredients in a cup or mug; stir well to dissolve honey.

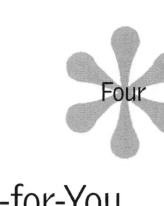

Four

Good-for-You Drinks

NOT ONLY are the drinks in this chapter low in fat and sugar, but they were chosen for their healthful components. You can boost the nutrient content of almost any drink with any of the following supplements:

❋ *Acidophilus* (1 tsp.) to help balance the intestinal tract's healthy bacteria.

❋ *Algae—spirulina, chlorella,* and so on (1 tsp.), a rich source of trace minerals and beta-carotene.

✳ *Brewer's Yeast* (1 Tbsp.), an excellent source of chromium and B vitamins; good for energy production.

✳ *Calcium (liquid)* (1 Tbsp.) for bone stability.

✳ *Flaxseed* (oil—1 tsp.; powder—1 Tbsp.), a good source of soluble and insoluble fiber and of the essential fatty acid linolenic acid.

✳ *Lecithin Granules* (1 Tbsp.) for the memory and proper liver function.

✳ *Propolis* (1 Tbsp.) for stimulating the immune system.

✳ *Psyllium Powder* (1 tsp.), a rich source of soluble fiber.

✳ *Soy Protein Powder* (1 Tbsp.) to balance carbohydrates and insulin.

✳ *Vitamin C Powder* (1 tsp.), a powerful antioxidant.

✳ *Wheat Germ* (1 Tbsp.), a rich source of protein, fiber, and vitamin E.

Sassy Redhead

Tomatoes contain lycopene, a strong antioxidant touted as a cancer fighter. They're also rich in vitamin C and contain appreciable amounts of vitamins A and B, potassium, iron, and phosphorus. Research shows that daily servings of tomato paste will keep us heart-healthy. Here's a good start toward that goal.

SERVES 1

½ cup (4 oz.) buttermilk
½ cup (4 oz.) tomato juice
½ cup silken tofu
3 Tbsp. tomato paste
1 tsp. chopped fresh dill or tarragon, or ¼ tsp.
    dried dill weed or tarragon
dash of Tabasco sauce (optional)
3 ice cubes, coarsely crushed
salt and freshly ground pepper

Combine all ingredients except salt and pepper in a
blender. Cover and process at medium speed until
smooth. Season to taste with salt and pepper. Pour into
a tall glass.

✳ **A cooked tomato is like a cooked oyster:
ruined.**

—André Simon, French gastronome

Gazpachito (gahz-pah-CHEE-toh)

This flavorful gazpacho smoothie is chock-full of vitamins and minerals. At the height of summer, when tomatoes are rife, make and freeze batches of this recipe to
enjoy as a tonic during the winter doldrums.

SERVES 4 TO 6

4 large, ripe red tomatoes, quartered
1 small onion, quartered
1 medium cucumber, peeled and cut into large
    chunks
1 small green pepper, seeded and cut into
    chunks
½ cup coarsely chopped radishes
2 to 3 large garlic cloves, peeled
1 Tbsp. (½ oz.) fresh lemon juice
1½ tsp. chopped fresh tarragon or ¾ tsp. dried
    tarragon leaves
¼ to ½ tsp. cayenne pepper
salt and freshly ground pepper
tomato juice (optional)
4 to 6 lemon slices

In 2 or 3 batches, combine tomatoes, onion, cucumber, green pepper, radishes, garlic, lemon juice, tarragon, and cayenne in a blender. Cover and process at medium-high speed until smooth. Strain each batch through a fine sieve (or a regular sieve lined with a double layer of cheesecloth), pressing down with the back of a spoon to extract all the liquid; discard solids. Salt and pepper to taste. If mixture is too thick, thin with tomato juice. Serve in tall, ice-filled glasses; garnish with lemon slices.

VARIATIONS

Gazpachito Verde (Green Gazpachito)   Substitute green or yellow tomatoes for the red tomatoes.

Gazpachito Caliente (Hot Gazpachito)   Heat over medium-low heat until simmering. Pour into warm mugs; float lemon slices on top.

Tomato Sunrise

The combination of tomato, orange, and lime juices gives this rejuvenator a megadose of vitamin C.

SERVES 8

1 46-oz. can chilled tomato juice
2 cups (16 oz.) fresh orange juice
½ cup (4 oz.) fresh lime juice (6 to 7 limes)
1 tsp. ground allspice
1 tsp. ground cumin
½ tsp. Tabasco sauce (optional)
salt and freshly ground pepper (optional)
8 lime slices for garnish

In a large pitcher, combine all ingredients except salt, pepper, and garnish; stir well. Taste for seasoning; add salt and pepper, if desired. Pour into tall glasses, each filled with 3 to 4 ice cubes; garnish with lime slices.

Blondie

Passion fruit is loaded with vitamins A and C—and you already know what tomatoes can do for you. Serve this exotic-tasting libation at your next brunch and no one will know they're getting a nutritional boost.

SERVES 4

4 medium yellow tomatoes, cored and
   quartered
1 cup (8 oz.) passion fruit nectar
¼ cup (2 oz.) fresh lime juice
¼ cup mint leaves
2 Tbsp. (1 oz.) honey
½ tsp. ground ginger
¼ tsp. freshly grated nutmeg
¼ tsp. ground cinnamon
8 ice cubes, coarsely crushed
salt
4 slices star fruit (carambola) for
   garnish

Combine all ingredients except ice, salt, and garnish in a blender. Cover and process at high speed until smooth. Add crushed ice cubes; process 15 seconds (ice will break into large chunks). Salt to taste. Pour into 4 medium-size stemmed glasses; garnish with star fruit slices.

Frozen Assets

L EE JANVRIN, a dear friend, has a technique for savoring an overabundant summer tomato harvest in the middle of winter: Put fresh-picked, ripe but firm, cored but *unwashed* tomatoes in a freezer-weight plastic bag and freeze until solid. When ready to use, briefly run the frozen tomato under lukewarm (not hot) water, which loosens the skin. (Don't thaw, or you'll lose much of the juice.) Use your fingers or a paring knife to pull off the skin, then add the frozen tomato to a smoothie, sauce, soup, or any other preparation in which you would normally use puréed tomatoes (freezing breaks down the tomato's cells so that they don't hold their shape).

Apricot Gingeraid

The soothing combination of apricots and ginger comes to the aid of anyone suffering from mental or physical fatigue or stress. Nutrient-rich apricots are high in beta-carotene (which converts to vitamin A in the body) and contain good amounts of iron, potassium, magnesium, and copper. Look for organically dried apricots, which have less sodium than those treated with sodium sulfur.

SERVES 4

2 cups (16 oz.) water
1 cup packed dried apricot halves
1-inch piece (½ inch in diameter) peeled ginger,
    thinly sliced
2 Tbsp. (1 oz.) honey
½ tsp. ground ginger
½ tsp. ground allspice
½ tsp. ground cinnamon
about 2 cups (16 oz.) chilled ginger ale

In a medium saucepan, combine water, apricots, ginger, honey, and ground spices; bring to a boil. Reduce heat to low; cover and simmer 10 minutes. Let stand until room temperature, or refrigerate until chilled. Turn apricot mixture into a blender. Cover and blend at high speed until smooth. Divide between 4 glasses. Add 3 ice cubes to each; top with ginger ale, stirring gently.

VARIATION

Hot Apricot Gingeraid   Let cooked apricots stand, covered, for 15 minutes. Blend as directed; start cautiously at low speed and gradually increase speed to high so hot liquid doesn't explode out of blender. Return mixture to saucepan; stir in ginger ale. Cook over medium heat, stirring occasionally, until mixture begins to simmer. Pour into warm mugs; garnish each serving with a dried apricot, if desired.

Ginger Power

GINGER IS a remarkable spice. Not only does it lend an exotic flavor to myriad foods and drinks, but its medicinal qualities have been prized for eons. Modern-day science confirms that ginger contains many healing qualities—it's an antioxidant and an anti-inflammatory; it relieves nausea, thins the blood, and destroys bacteria. A natural remedy that tastes great—what a concept!

Gingerberry Buzz

Make this the day before to allow the flavors to mingle.

SERVES 4

3 cups (24 oz.) water
2 cups (16 oz.) cranberry juice
1 cup fresh cranberries
½ cup peeled, thinly sliced ginger
½ cup sugar
5 whole cloves
about 1 cup (8 oz.) chilled seltzer water or club soda (optional)
12 fresh cranberries for garnish

In a medium saucepan, combine water, cranberry juice, cranberries, ginger, sugar, and cloves; bring to a boil.

Cover and simmer 5 minutes. Remove from heat; cool to room temperature. Refrigerate overnight or until very cold. Strain into a pitcher; serve in tall, ice-filled glasses. Add a splash of seltzer, if desired; float 3 cranberries in each glass.

VARIATION

Hot Gingerberry Buzz   Let ingredients steep in hot liquid for at least 1 hour. Reheat until simmering; strain into warm mugs. *See also* Tips for Making Hot Drinks, page 184.

Cranberry Cream

Cranberries are very high in vitamin C and a great aid in urinary-tract health.

SERVES 1

½ cup chilled whole-berry cranberry sauce
¾ to 1 cup (6 to 8 oz.) chilled orange or
   strawberry-orange yogurt
½ cup (4 oz.) chilled cranberry or orange juice
orange wedge for garnish

Combine all ingredients except garnish in a blender. Cover and process at high speed until smooth. Pour into a tall glass; garnish with orange wedge.

Morning Glory

This great morning eye-opener will wake up your groggy head and provide fuel for the rest of the day.

SERVES 1

¾ cup (6 oz.) soymilk

¾ cup (6 oz.) fresh orange juice

½ tsp. pure vanilla extract

1 Tbsp. toasted wheat germ or oat bran

1 egg or ¼ cup egg substitute (optional)

Combine all ingredients in a blender. Cover and process at medium speed until smooth. Pour into a tall glass.

 Only dull people are brilliant at breakfast.

—Oscar Wilde, Anglo-Irish playwright, critic

Golden Girl

This refreshing golden drink has an exotic, not overly sweet flavor. Carrots are rich in vitamin A and contain many other nutrients, including B vitamins, phosphorus, iodine, and calcium.

SERVES 2

¾ cup (6 oz.) chilled carrot juice
¾ cup (6 oz.) low-fat coconut milk
¾ to 1 cup (6 to 8 oz.) orange yogurt
2 Tbsp. (1 oz.) honey (optional)
pinch of salt
2 carrot curls for garnish

Combine all ingredients except garnish in a blender. Cover and process at medium speed until smooth. Pour into tall glasses; garnish with carrot curls.

 **Some claim that ginseng is the best,
The miracle begetter
But carrots cost a whole lot less
and taste a wee bit better.**

—James Duke, American botanist

Cucumber Crave

Ever wonder where the phrase "cool as a cucumber" comes from? Probably from the fact that a cucumber's internal temperature is always several degrees cooler than the atmosphere. That's because a cucumber contains about 90 percent water, which translates to a very slim calorie count of around 40 for a medium cuke. Filling, satisfying, and low in calories and sodium—perfect for dieters!

SERVES 6

4 cups (32 oz.) buttermilk
2 medium cucumbers, peeled, seeded, and
   coarsely chopped
½ cup packed fresh mint leaves or ¼ cup snipped
   fresh dill weed
¼ cup (2 oz.) fresh lime juice
2 cups crushed ice
salt and pepper
6 mint sprigs or unpeeled cucumber slices for
   garnish

Combine 2 cups of the buttermilk, 1 cucumber, and mint or dill in a blender. Cover and process at high speed until smooth. Pour into a pitcher. Blend remaining 2 cups buttermilk, remaining cucumber, and lime juice until smooth; pour into pitcher. Add crushed ice and salt and pepper to taste; stir vigorously. Pour into tall glasses; garnish with mint sprigs or cucumber slices.

✳ **I want nothing to do with natural foods. At my age I need all the preservatives I can get.**

—George Burns, American actor, comedian

Papaya Pick-Me-Up

The nutrient-dense papaya contains almost three times the amount of vitamins C and A than the recommended daily allowances. Combined with the vitamin C and antioxidants in strawberries, you have a nutrition-packed breakfast or lunch smoothie.

SERVES 2

1 papaya, peeled, seeded, and coarsely chopped
1 cup sliced strawberries
1 cup (8 oz.) soymilk or rice milk
2 Tbsp. (1 oz.) fresh lime juice
4 ice cubes, coarsely crushed
2 whole strawberries for garnish

Combine all ingredients except garnish in a blender. Cover and process at high speed until smooth. Pour into tall glasses; garnish with strawberries.

VARIATION

Papaya-Orange Pick-Me-Up　Substitute fresh orange juice for the soy or rice milk; garnish with orange slices.

Bossa Nova

This exotic drink is named after the Brazilian musical blend of jazz and samba. Half an 8-ounce avocado contains only about 70 calories and is rich in heart-healthy monounsaturated fats.

SERVES 1

½ avocado, pitted, peeled, and quartered
1 cup (8 oz.) pineapple juice
½ cup (4 oz.) low-fat coconut milk
1 Tbsp. (½ oz.) fresh lime juice
¼ tsp. freshly grated nutmeg
lime wedge for garnish (optional)

Combine all ingredients except garnish in a blender. Cover and process at high speed until smooth. Pour into a tall glass; garnish with lime wedge, if desired.

Food for Thought

THE AVOCADO'S name comes from *ahuacatl,* the Nahuatl word for "testicle," presumably in reference to the shape of the fruit.

Dream Date

This is a wonderful soother for frazzled nerves. Dates are high in fiber and are a source of calcium, magnesium, and folic acid. Rehydrate dry dates before using by covering them with boiling water and letting stand for 30 minutes.

SERVES 1

¾ cup (6 oz.) soymilk, almond milk, or rice milk
½ cup (4 oz.) plain or vanilla yogurt
⅓ cup pitted dates, coarsely chopped
1 small ripe banana, peeled and quartered
1 tsp. ground ginger

Combine all ingredients in a blender. Cover and process at high speed until smooth. Pour into a tall glass.

VARIATION

Pineapple Dream Date   Substitute pineapple juice for the almond milk, rice milk, or soymilk.

Pumpkin Pie Pleaser

You've heard of having your cake and eating it, too? Well, now you can have your pumpkin pie with the added nutrition of soy and without all the calories.

SERVES 1

¾ cup (6 oz.) soymilk
⅔ cup pumpkin purée
⅓ cup silken tofu
2 to 3 Tbsp. (1 to 1½ oz.) pure maple syrup
½ tsp. pure vanilla extract

1 tsp. pumpkin pie spice or ¼ tsp. *each* cinnamon,
ginger, nutmeg, and allspice

Combine all ingredients in a blender. Cover and process
at medium speed until smooth. Pour into a tall glass.

✳ **My favorite word is "pumpkin." ... You can't
take it seriously. But you can't ignore it either.
It takes ahold of your heart and that's it. You
are a pumpkin. Or you are not. I am.**
—Harrison Salisbury, American journalist

Barley Water

This is an old English restorative and remedy for everything from coughs to gastritis. Unrefined (or pot) barley is
more nutritious than pearl barley. It can be found in natural food stores, whereas pearl barley is available in most
supermarkets. Use the reserved cooked barley in smoothies, soups, or stir-fry dishes. If the barley is to be used in a
savory dish, strain it first, then add the honey with the
lemon juice.

MAKES ABOUT 2½ CUPS

3 cups (24 oz.) water
½ cup unrefined or pearl barley

grated zest and juice of 1 medium lemon
2 to 3 Tbsp. (1 to 1½ oz.) honey

In a medium saucepan, combine water, barley, and lemon zest; bring to a boil. Reduce heat to low; cover and simmer 30 minutes. Remove from heat; stir in honey. Let cool to room temperature. Strain liquid into a container with a tight lid; reserve barley for another use. Stir lemon juice into barley liquid. Seal tightly and refrigerate for up to a week. Serve at room temperature or lukewarm in cups or small glasses. May be added to other drinks in place of other liquids.

Five

Smoothies

I N THE MOST basic terms, a smoothie is a fruit- or vegetable-based drink combined with juice, yogurt, or another mixer and made smooth by blending. An electric blender is the machine of choice here—food processors don't do the job as well and often leak. You'll get the best results by starting to blend at low speed and gradually increasing to high speed.

It's hard to go wrong with a smoothie. If it's too thick, add liquid and blend again; too thin, add more fruit. For a milkshake consistency, use frozen fruit. Want more nutrition and fewer calories? Use soymilk, buttermilk, silken tofu, or yogurt. Starting with chilled ingredients means you won't have to dilute the mix with ice. On the other hand, if it's wintertime and you can't bear the thought of something chilly, use room-temperature ingredients.

Eve's Apple

Leaving the peel on the apples adds fiber, but be sure and wash the apples well. The orange-flower water lends an exotic touch.

SERVES 2

1½ cups (12 oz.) chilled, fresh orange juice
2 medium apples, cored and coarsely chopped
    (peeling optional)
2 Tbsp. packed brown sugar
½ tsp. ground allspice
½ tsp. orange-flower water
pinch of salt
2 apple wedges for garnish

Combine 1 cup of the orange juice, apples, sugar, allspice, orange-flower water, and salt in a blender. Cover and process at high speed until smooth. Add remaining ½ cup juice; blend to combine. Pour into tall glasses; garnish with apple wedges.

Myth Conception

W E A L L K N O W that the forbidden fruit Eve offered Adam was an apple, right? Well, archaeologists say that's not probable—apples didn't grow in the Middle East when Genesis is thought to have been written. And the Bible describes the tree of knowledge as: " . . . good for food and pleasant to the eyes, and a tree to be desired to make one wise." Not exactly specific. The more likely object of temptation according to many scholars? A luscious apricot.

Apricot-Mango Mania

For a more tropical flavor you can substitute passion fruit nectar for the apricot nectar.

SERVES 2

2 medium mangoes, peeled and diced
¾ to 1 cup (6 to 8 oz.) apricot-mango, apricot, or
    vanilla yogurt
⅔ cup (scant 6 oz.) apricot nectar
1 Tbsp. (½ oz.) fresh lime juice
½ tsp. ground ginger
5 ice cubes, coarsely crushed

Combine all ingredients in a blender. Cover and process at high speed until smooth. Pour into tall glasses.

✳ **When I have eaten mangoes,
I have felt like Eve.**

—Rose Macaulay, British novelist

Honey-Butter Smoothie

Partially freezing the bananas beforehand gives this drink a silky texture.

SERVES 2

1 cup (8 oz.) milk
2 medium ripe bananas, peeled and quartered
⅓ cup creamy peanut butter
2 to 3 Tbsp. (1 to 1½ oz.) honey

Combine all ingredients in a blender. Cover and process at high speed until smooth. Pour into tall glasses.

VARIATION

Chocolate Honey-Butter Smoothie   Add ⅓ cup (ample 2½ oz.) Dark Chocolate Syrup, page 256, or store-bought chocolate syrup.

Hawaiian Hug

For a less sweet drink, substitute coconut milk for the cream of coconut.

SERVES 1

½ small ripe papaya, seeded, peeled, and coarsely
chopped
½ cup (4 oz.) chilled guava nectar
½ cup (4 oz.) chilled mango nectar
1 to 2 Tbsp. (½ to 1 oz.) cream of coconut
6 ice cubes, coarsely crushed
papaya slice or toasted coconut, page 259, for
garnish

Combine all ingredients except garnish in a blender.
Cover and process at high speed until smooth. Pour into
a tall glass; garnish with papaya slice or toasted
coconut.

Blue Sky Smoothie

Lemonade in lieu of orange juice gives this smoothie a slightly tarter flavor.

SERVES 4

1½ cups (12 oz.) fresh orange juice
2 cups (16 oz.) blueberry yogurt

1 medium ripe banana, peeled and quartered
1 pint fresh or 2 cups partially thawed, frozen
   blueberries, divided

Combine orange juice, yogurt, banana, and 1¾ cups of
the blueberries in a blender. Cover and process at
medium speed until smooth. Pour into tall
glasses. Sprinkle each serving with about 1 Tbsp.
of the remaining blueberries; serve with an
iced-tea spoon.

 On the strawberry:
Doubtless God could have made a better berry,
but doubtless God never did.
—William Butler, English novelist, essayist

Strawberries and Cream

Sometimes even strawberry lovers don't like all the little
seeds. If that includes you, purée and strain the berries
before adding the rest of the smoothie ingredients.

SERVES 2

1 pint strawberries, washed and hulled (reserve 2
   unhulled berries for garnish)

1 cup (8 oz.) strawberry yogurt
¾ cup (6 oz.) milk
2 Tbsp. (1 oz.) honey
⅛ tsp. freshly grated nutmeg

Combine all ingredients in a blender. Cover and process at high speed until smooth. Pour into tall glasses; garnish with reserved whole strawberries.

VARIATION

Blueberries and Cream   Substitute blueberries for strawberries, blueberry yogurt for strawberry yogurt, and maple syrup for the honey.

Banavalanche

Strawberry-banana or blueberry yogurt is also wonderful in this easy smoothie.

SERVES 1

1 medium ripe banana, peeled and quartered
¾ to 1 cup (6 to 8 oz.) banana or vanilla yogurt
⅓ cup (scant 3 oz.) fresh orange juice
pinch of ground allspice

Combine all ingredients in a blender. Cover and process at medium speed until smooth. Pour into a tall glass.

Coconut-Mango Twister

Papaya fans can substitute a small, seeded papaya for the mango for a variation on a theme.

SERVES 2

1 large mango, peeled and diced
1 medium ripe banana, peeled and
   quartered
¾ cup (6 oz.) chilled low-fat coconut milk
1 Tbsp. (½ oz.) fresh lime juice
4 ice cubes, coarsely crushed
toasted coconut, page 259, for garnish

Combine all ingredients except garnish in a blender. Cover and process at high speed until smooth. Pour into tall glasses; sprinkle with toasted coconut.

Pineapple-Papaya Smash

Try tossing a tablespoon of papaya seeds into the mix before blending—they'll add a slightly peppery taste that's bound to mystify all but the initiated.

SERVES 1

1 cup (8 oz.) chilled pineapple juice
1 medium papaya, peeled, seeded, and coarsely
   chopped
1 Tbsp. (½ oz.) fresh lime juice

1 Tbsp. (½ oz.) honey

3 ice cubes, coarsely crushed

Combine all ingredients in a blender. Cover and process at high speed until smooth. Pour into a tall glass.

✳ **The flavor of the raspberry stamps it "Made in Asia." It breathes of the Orient—rich, exotic, spice-laden and with a hint of musk.**

—Waverly Root, American writer

Peach Melba Mambo

This drink is named in honor of the classic dessert of poached peach halves, ice cream, and raspberry sauce. If fresh peaches aren't in season, partially thawed frozen peaches may be used—but taste them first, as some frozen peaches have very little flavor.

SERVES 2

1 cup raspberries

½ cup (4 oz.) milk

1 cup chopped, peeled peaches

1 cup (8 oz.) peach or raspberry yogurt

Reserve 6 raspberries for garnish. Combine remaining raspberries and milk in a blender. Cover and process at

high speed until smooth. Strain raspberry mixture
through a fine sieve into a small bowl or glass
measuring cup; press down on fruit to extract as much
liquid as possible. Rinse out blender jar before filling
with raspberry mixture, peaches, and yogurt. Blend at
high speed until smooth. Pour into tall glasses; garnish
with reserved raspberries.

Spiced Smoothie Spritz

Partner your palate with your imagination to personalize
this refresher by using your favorite yogurt, fresh fruit,
and spices.

SERVES 1

½ cup (4 oz.) plain or fruit-flavored yogurt
1 cup chopped fresh fruit
pinch of ground nutmeg, allspice, or
    cinnamon
about ½ cup (4 oz.) chilled seltzer water, club
    soda, or ginger ale
mint sprig or fruit slice for garnish (optional)

Combine first 3 ingredients in a blender. Cover and
process at high speed until smooth. Pour into a tall, ice-
filled glass. Top with seltzer, club soda, or ginger ale,
stirring gently. Garnish with mint sprig or fruit slice, if
desired.

Frosted Melon Frappé

Put two wineglasses in the freezer an hour beforehand to add a frosty touch.

SERVES 2

¾ to 1 cup (6 to 8 oz.) plain yogurt
2 rounded cups chilled cantaloupe or
   honeydew melon chunks (about 1 small
   melon)
2 Tbsp. superfine sugar
¾ tsp. pure vanilla extract
4 ice cubes, coarsely crushed
2 mint sprigs for garnish (optional)

Combine all ingredients except garnish in a blender. Cover and process at high speed until smooth. Pour into glasses; garnish with mint sprigs, if desired.

✳ **Adam was but human—this explains it all. He did not want the apple for the apple's sake, he wanted it only because it was forbidden.**

—Mark Twain, American author, humorist

Apple-Ginger Snap

For extra-spicy flavor, use cinnamon-flavored applesauce.

SERVES 1

½ cup (4 oz.) chilled fresh orange juice
½ cup gingersnap crumbs
1 cup chilled applesauce
¼ tsp. pure almond extract
ground ginger
apple wedge for garnish (optional)

Combine orange juice and gingersnaps in a blender. Cover and process at high speed for 10 seconds to soften cookie crumbs. Add applesauce and almond extract; process at high speed until smooth. Pour into a tall glass; sprinkle with ginger and hook apple wedge over glass rim, if desired.

Sunberry Smoothie

It's best to make this refresher in the summer, when berries are bountiful. For winter enjoyment, use partially thawed dry-pack berries.

SERVES 1

1 cup (8 oz.) strawberry, raspberry, or blueberry yogurt
1 cup mixed berries (blueberries, strawberries, and
  so on)
⅓ cup (scant 3 oz.) orange juice

Combine all ingredients in a blender. Cover and process at high speed until smooth. Pour into a tall glass.

Banana Colada

A banana bonus makes this piña colada–style smoothie special.

SERVES 1

1 large ripe banana, peeled and quartered
½ cup drained crushed pineapple in juice
½ cup (4 oz.) chilled low-fat coconut milk
¼ tsp. pure vanilla extract
3 ice cubes, coarsely crushed
banana slice or toasted coconut, page 259, for
garnish

Combine all ingredients except garnish in a blender. Cover and process at high speed until smooth. Pour into a large, tall glass. Garnish with banana slice or toasted coconut.

Pink Piñata

Be sure to buy crushed pineapple packed in juice—the syrup-packed version will make this drink too sweet.

SERVES 2

1 8-oz. can crushed pineapple in juice (don't drain)
1 pint strawberries, washed and hulled (reserve 2
unhulled berries for garnish)

4 ice cubes, coarsely crushed

4 Tbsp. (2 oz.) half & half or cream

Combine pineapple and its juice, strawberries, ice, and 2 Tbsp. of the half & half in a blender. Cover and process at high speed until smooth. If smoothie is too thick, add additional half & half and blend again. Pour into tall glasses; garnish with reserved whole berries.

Mango Swizzle

Seltzer water adds sass to this smoothie. Lime-flavored sparkling water can be used in its place.

SERVES 6

2 medium mangoes, peeled, seeded, and coarsely chopped

2 cups (16 oz.) fresh orange juice

¼ cup (2 oz.) fresh lime or lemon juice

¼ cup superfine sugar

about 2 cups (16 oz.) chilled seltzer water or club soda

6 orange slices for garnish

Combine all ingredients except seltzer and garnish in a blender. Cover and process at high speed until smooth. Divide equally between 6 tall glasses; add 2 or 3 ice cubes to each. Top with seltzer, stirring gently; garnish with orange slices.

Papaya-Passion Fling

SERVES 1

½ cup (4 oz.) passion fruit nectar
¾ to 1 cup (6 to 8 oz.) vanilla yogurt
½ small papaya, peeled, seeded, and coarsely
chopped
¼ tsp. ground allspice

Combine all ingredients in a blender. Cover and process at high speed until smooth. Pour into a tall glass; serve with a straw.

Fresh Fruit Bubble Drink

If you're up on current trends, you'll know what bubble drinks are. If not, you can read about them in the section on Bubble Tea, page 174.

SERVES 1

⅓ cup cooked Tapioca Pearls, page 175
¾ cup (6 oz.) milk
1 cup chopped fresh fruit
6 ice cubes, coarsely crushed
Sugar Syrup, page 251, or superfine sugar
to taste

Spoon tapioca pearls into a large, tall glass. Combine remaining ingredients in a blender. Cover and process at high speed until smooth. Pour into glass over pearls; serve with fat straw.

VARIATION

Tropical Bubble Drink   Substitute low-fat coconut milk for the milk and use 1 cup canned, drained litchi (lychee) nuts (available in Asian markets and some supermarkets) or fresh papaya or mango for the fruit.

Six

Frosty Pleasers

Milkshakes, Malts, and
Other Frosty Teasers

ID YOU know that milk-
shakes were once relatively
simple, wholesome blends of
milk and flavored syrup?
Seems hard to reconcile that
drink with the ice cream–dominant blend
that is today's milkshake. Still, it's difficult
to argue the allure of the thick, rich, creamy
concoctions that sing a siren song to so
many of us, particularly on hot summer
days. Of course, no one's saying you have to
use premium ice cream for such concoctions. Low-fat or sugar-free styles are
perfectly acceptable and will be kinder to

your waistline. But they won't have that soul-stirring, toe-tapping satisfaction that the fattening versions deliver.

Ice cream and sherbet will blend better with other ingredients if they're slightly softened first. This can be done in one of two ways: Either let the ice cream or sherbet stand at room temperature for about 20 minutes or microwave at MEDIUM-LOW (30 percent) power. A quart of ice cream will take about 30 seconds, a pint slightly less. Low-fat ice creams and frozen yogurts melt faster than their caloric cousins.

The ice cream scoop I used for the recipes in this book contains 3 fluid ounces. To check your scoop size, fill it with water and then measure the amount it holds. On average, you can count on about five 3-ounce scoops of ice cream per pint. Spray an ice cream scoop with nonstick vegetable spray and the ice cream will slip right out.

 **Lead me not into temptation;
I can find the way myself.**

—Rita Mae Brown, American author

Malted Milkshake

You can make any shake into a "malted" by adding 1 to 2 tablespoons of malted milk powder to the ingredients

before blending. Horlicks brand malt powder has a nice,
clean flavor. Malt has a particular affinity with
chocolate.

Maple-Pecan Frostee

For the best flavor, use pure maple syrup for this shake—
bland-tasting "pancake" syrup (artificially flavored corn
syrup) will deliver little more than sweetness.

SERVES 2

¾ cup (6 oz.) milk
⅓ cup (scant 3 oz.) pure maple syrup
5 scoops butter pecan ice cream, slightly
   softened
freshly grated nutmeg for garnish

Combine all ingredients except garnish in a blender.
Cover and process at medium speed until smooth. Pour
into tall glasses; dust with nutmeg. Serve with straws
and iced-tea spoons.

VARIATION

Caramel-Pecan Frostee Substitute Ooey-Gooey
Caramel Sauce, page 257, or store-bought caramel
sauce for the maple syrup; garnish with a drizzle of
caramel sauce.

Cheesecake Shake

This couldn't be easier to make, or more delicious. The secret ingredient is buttermilk, which produces that tangy cheesecake flavor (and which no one will guess is there!).

SERVES 1

¾ cup (6 oz.) buttermilk

3 scoops vanilla ice cream, slightly softened

⅛ tsp. pure vanilla extract

1 to 2 tsp. graham cracker crumbs for garnish (optional)

Combine all ingredients except garnish in a blender. Cover and process at medium speed until smooth. Pour into a tall glass; sprinkle with graham cracker crumbs, if desired.

VARIATIONS

Chocolate Cheesecake Shake   Substitute chocolate ice cream for the vanilla ice cream.

Fruit Cheesecake Shake   Substitute any fruit-flavored ice cream (strawberry, peach, and so on) for the vanilla ice cream.

 Research tells us that fourteen out of any ten individuals like chocolate.

—Sandra Boynton, American illustrator, songwriter, author

Serious Chocolate Shake

The secret to a truly wonderful chocolate shake is in the chocolate syrup. Sure, you can buy the syrup, but when making your own is so easy, why bother?

SERVES 1

¼ cup (2 oz.) milk

⅓ cup (scant 3 oz.) Dark Chocolate Syrup, page 256, or store-bought chocolate syrup

3 scoops vanilla ice cream, slightly softened

whipped cream for garnish (optional)

grated chocolate for garnish (optional)

Combine all ingredients except garnishes in a blender. Cover and process at medium speed until smooth. Pour into a tall glass. If desired, garnish with a dollop of whipped cream sprinkled with grated chocolate. Serve with a straw and an iced-tea spoon.

VARIATIONS

Double Chocolate Shake   Substitute chocolate ice cream for the vanilla ice cream.

Black Forest Shake   Add ¼ cup cherry preserves before blending.

> ✳ **For generations, it has been as American as apple pie to want a piece of the pie, even though getting it might not be as easy as pie. . . .**
> —Jay Jacobs, American author, food critic

Frosty Apple Pie à la Mode

Never did cold "pie" taste so wonderful.

SERVES 2

½ cup (4 oz.) milk
1 cup canned apple pie filling
¼ tsp. *each* ground allspice and freshly grated
    nutmeg
4 scoops vanilla ice cream, slightly softened
freshly grated nutmeg for garnish

Combine milk, pie filling, and spices in a blender. Cover and process at high speed until smooth. Add ice cream; blend at medium speed until smooth. Pour into tall glasses; garnish with a dusting of nutmeg.

VARIATIONS

Candied Apple Pie à la Mode Add ¼ cup red-hot cinnamon candies with the ice cream.

Caramel Apple Pie à la Mode Substitute caramel or caramel-swirl ice cream for the vanilla ice cream; drizzle top with caramel sauce.

Orange Juliana

A home rendition of the famous Orange Julius. The egg whites give this drink its foamy texture.

SERVES 4 TO 5

1 6-oz. can frozen orange juice concentrate,
    unthawed
4 cups (32 oz.) chilled water
½ cup nonfat dry milk powder
⅔ cup superfine sugar
2 egg whites or ¼ cup (2 oz.) egg substitute
1½ tsp. pure vanilla extract
about 2 cups ice cubes, coarsely crushed

Combine all ingredients except ice in a blender. Cover and process at high speed for 15 seconds. Add crushed ice cubes, a handful at a time, blending until mixture is smooth and reaches desired thickness. Serve in tall glasses with straws.

I doubt the world holds for anyone a more soul-stirring surprise than the first adventure with ice cream.

—Heywood Broun, American journalist, novelist

Funky Monkey

One taste and you'll feel like a kid again. Chocolate-loving "kids" will love the Fudgy Funky Monkey variation.

SERVES 2

½ cup (4 oz.) milk
2 small ripe bananas, peeled and quartered
⅓ cup creamy peanut butter
¼ tsp. ground cinnamon
3 scoops vanilla or peanut butter ice cream,
    slightly softened

Combine all ingredients except ice cream in a blender. Cover and process at high speed until smooth. Add ice cream; blend at medium speed until smooth. Pour into tall glasses; serve with straws and iced-tea spoons.

VARIATION

Fudgy Funky Monkey   Substitute dark chocolate ice cream for the vanilla ice cream; add ¼ cup (2 oz.) Dark Chocolate Syrup, page 256, or store-bought chocolate syrup.

Dreamsicle

A takeoff on my favorite childhood frozen bar. For a completely different but equally delicious drink, substitute orange sherbet for the vanilla ice cream.

SERVES 2

½ cup (4 oz.) frozen orange juice concentrate,
    unthawed
¾ cup (6 oz.) milk
¾ tsp. pure vanilla extract
5 scoops vanilla ice cream, slightly softened
2 orange slices for garnish

Combine first 3 ingredients in a blender. Cover and process at high speed for 5 seconds. Add ice cream; cover and process at medium speed until smooth. Pour into tall glasses; garnish with orange slices. Serve with straws and iced-tea spoons.

Vanilla Splash

For exotic flavor and pure comfort, it's hard to beat this easy pleaser. I love the silky texture of vanilla gelato in this drink.

SERVES 1

2 scoops vanilla ice cream or gelato, slightly
    softened
2 tsp. pure vanilla extract

about ¾ cup (6 oz.) chilled seltzer water or club
soda

Place 1 scoop of the ice cream and the vanilla in the
bottom of a tall glass. Use a long-handled spoon to
lightly blend the ingredients together. Add second scoop
of ice cream; top with seltzer, stirring gently. Serve with
a straw and an iced-tea spoon.

Ice Cream—It Could Be a Lot of Cold Air

ALL COMMERCIAL ice creams contain a certain
amount of air, called "overrun" in the ice cream
industry. The percentage of overrun ranges from 0 (no
air) to 200 (all air), the latter a dieter's delight. In the
United States, ice cream's legal overrun limit is 100
percent (half air), though such a blend would be mushy
and melt exceedingly fast. Naturally, ice cream needs
some air or it would be rock hard, and the usual overrun
range is from 20 to 50 percent. Since the overrun
percentage isn't listed on ice cream labels, the only way
to calculate how much air you're paying for is to weigh
the package. Ice cream with 50 percent overrun (25
percent air) will weigh about 18 ounces per pint (sub-
tract about 1½ ounces for the container). Bottom line:
The less overrun, the more a pint of ice cream will weigh.

Fresh Fruit Slushy

Make these drinks an hour ahead of time so they get good and slushy. Fruit-flavored yogurt (the same flavor as the fresh fruit) may be substituted for the plain or vanilla yogurt.

SERVES 2

1 cup (8 oz.) plain or vanilla yogurt
1½ cups chopped fresh fruit
½ cup (4 oz.) milk
2 to 3 Tbsp. superfine sugar

Combine all ingredients in a blender. Cover and process at high speed until smooth. Pour into medium-size stemmed glasses. Place in freezer until slushy, or about an hour. Stir before serving.

✳ **We dare not trust our wit for making our house pleasant to our friends, so we buy ice cream.**
—Ralph Waldo Emerson, American poet, philosopher, essayist

Mandarin Pillow

This exotic mélange is the perfect ending for a company dinner. If you don't have time to make or shop for the coffee-flavored syrup, substitute ½ cup chilled strong coffee mixed with ½ cup superfine sugar.

1 11-oz. can mandarin oranges, thoroughly drained
½ cup (4 oz.) chilled Coffee Syrup, page 252, or
    store-bought coffee-flavored syrup
1 quart vanilla ice cream, slightly softened
½ cup whipping cream, whipped and sweetened
    to taste
2 Tbsp. grated chocolate

Combine drained oranges and coffee syrup in a blender.
Cover and process at high speed until smooth. Add half
of the ice cream; blend at medium speed to combine.
Add remaining ice cream; blend until smooth. Pour into
medium-size stemmed glasses or brandy snifters.
Garnish each serving with a dollop of whipped cream,
sprinkled with grated chocolate. Serve with straws and
iced-tea spoons.

Black Cow

Black Cow is the midwestern U.S. term for a root beer
float. It's also variously known as "brown cow" (which can
also refer to a cola float) and "sassy cow." Chocoholics will
love the variation.

SERVES 1

2 scoops vanilla ice cream, slightly softened
about 1 cup (8 oz.) chilled root beer

whipped cream for garnish
maraschino cherry for garnish

Place ice cream in a tall glass. Gently add root beer, starting to pour on the side of the glass so the foam won't run over. Garnish with a dollop of whipped cream topped with a maraschino cherry. Serve with a straw and an iced-tea spoon.

VARIATIONS

Black Cow with a Kick   Place 1 scoop ice cream in a glass. Drizzle with 1 Tbsp. (½ oz.) Dark Chocolate Syrup, page 256, or store-bought chocolate syrup; use a spoon to lightly blend. Repeat with second scoop of ice cream and another tablespoon chocolate syrup. Add root beer, then whipped cream; garnish with grated chocolate.

Chocolate Black Cow   Substitute chocolate ice cream for the vanilla ice cream.

Brown Cow   Substitute cola for the root beer.

Kiss O' Citrus Soda

A sparkling kiss of citrus over your favorite ice cream or sherbet—what could be more refreshing? Use the same flavor sparkling water as the syrup (a lime-flavored water with lime syrup, and so on). Minted Citrus Syrup, page 255, makes a particularly nice combination with lemon-flavored water. You can also continue the flavor theme by using lemon sherbet.

SERVES 1

3 to 4 Tbsp. (1½ to 2 oz.) citrus-flavored syrup
(orange, lemon, lime, or grapefruit), store-
bought or homemade, pages 253–255
about 1 cup (8 oz.) chilled sparkling water
2 scoops vanilla ice cream or fruit-flavored
sherbet, slightly softened
mint sprig

In a tall glass, stir together the syrup and ⅓ cup of the sparkling water. Add ice cream; top with remaining sparkling water. Stir gently; garnish with mint sprig. Serve with a straw and an iced-tea spoon.

 Ice cream unleashes the uninhibited eight-year-old's sensual greed that lurks within the best of us.
—Gael Greene, American author, editor, restaurant critic

Fruit Juicy Shake

This easy shake has as many variations as there are combinations of juice and ice cream, frozen yogurt, or sherbet.

Some wonderful combination frozen juice concentrates are orange-peach-mango and guava-strawberry. Look for the Hawaii's Own brand, which produces several exotic blends.

SERVES 2

¾ cup (6 oz.) milk
1 6-oz. can frozen juice concentrate, unthawed
1 pint ice cream, frozen yogurt, or sherbet, slightly
    softened
fruit slice or wedge for garnish

Combine milk and juice concentrate in a blender. Cover and process at high speed until smooth. Add ice cream, 2 scoops at a time; blend at medium speed until smooth. Pour into tall glasses; garnish with fruit the same flavor as the juice. Serve with straws and iced-tea spoons.

VARIATIONS

Apple Annie   Apple juice concentrate, vanilla ice cream, and ¾ tsp. ground cinnamon. Garnish with apple slices.

Apple Butter Shake   Apple juice concentrate, butter-pecan or praline ice cream. Garnish with crushed praline candy.

Braziliana   Pineapple-banana-orange juice concentrate and mango, coconut, or orange sherbet.

Garnish with wedges of pineapple, banana, or orange and/or toasted coconut, page 259.

Café Olé Shake   Orange juice concentrate and coffee ice cream. Garnish with a dusting of instant coffee powder (not granules) and orange slices.

Berryluscious Shake   Cranberry-raspberry juice concentrate and vanilla ice cream. Garnish with a dusting of nutmeg.

Crazy for Cranberries   Cranberry juice concentrate and orange sherbet. Garnish with orange slices.

Orange-Chocolate Shake   Orange juice concentrate and chocolate ice cream. Garnish with orange wedges and grated chocolate.

Sassy Peach   Orange-peach-mango juice concentrate with peach ice cream. Garnish with orange or peach slices.

Purple Pleaser   Grape juice concentrate and lemon sherbet. Garnish with purple jelly beans.

Strawberry Splendor   Pineapple-orange-strawberry juice concentrate and strawberry ice cream. Garnish with whole strawberries.

Sunshine Shake   Pink grapefruit juice concentrate
and orange sherbet. Garnish with orange slices.

Tropicana   Pineapple juice concentrate, 1 peeled and
quartered banana, and macadamia nut or praline ice
cream. Garnish with toasted coconut, page 259, or
pineapple spears.

Seven

Coffee Drinks

✳ **Actually, this seems to be the basic need of the human heart in nearly every great crisis—a good cup of coffee.**

—Alexander King, American author

The Consummate Cup of Coffee

ARE YOU ONE of those people who just can't make a good cup of coffee? Following these tips guarantees success—or at least a better brew than you've been producing.

✻ Make sure the coffeepot and filter are absolutely clean. Residual coffee oils from previous brews can gather in nooks and crannies and contribute a bitter, rancid flavor.

✻ Use freshly drawn cold water, and remember that coffee will only be as good as the water with which it's made. Highly chlorinated or mineral-tasting water can produce bitter, off-tasting coffee. Use bottled water if necessary.

✻ Check your coffeemaker's instruction booklet and use the suggested amount, grind, and brewing time.

✻ For a full-flavored brew, use 2 level table-spoons (1 coffee measure; ⅛ cup) for each ¾ cup (6 ounces) of water. Keep in mind that a standard coffee cup holds 6 ounces, whereas a mug's capacity is often 10 to 12 ounces. For stronger coffee, use 2 level tablespoons for each ½ cup (4 ounces) of water.

✻ If your coffee tastes acidic, add a pinch of salt to the next batch of grounds before brewing.

✳ Coffee flavor begins to deteriorate within 15 minutes after it's brewed. Leaving the coffee on a heating element expedites the process—as the coffee sits there, aromatic oils evaporate, causing the brew to taste bitter and flat. Retain first-cup freshness by transferring coffee to a vacuum-insulated carafe that's been preheated with hot water.

✳ Coffee caveat: Reheating coffee just makes it bitter.

✳ **If you can make a good cup of coffee, you can make any man glad he has left his mother.**

—Mrs. W. T. Hayes, American cookbook author

Hot Coffee Drinks

Café Crème Brûlée [ka-fay krehm broo-LAY]

A drinkable coffee-flavored version of the creamy burnt-caramel classic (*brûlé* is French for "burned"). Sip this with someone special—guilty pleasures should be shared. *See also* Tips for Making Hot Drinks, page 184.

SERVES 2

½ cup sugar

2 Tbsp. (1 oz.) plus 1 cup (8 oz.) water

⅛ tsp. salt

2 Tbsp. instant espresso powder

1 cup (8 oz.) whipping cream or half & half

1 tsp. pure vanilla extract

additional sugar (optional)

whipped cream for garnish (optional)

2 orange twists

In a small, heavy saucepan, combine sugar, 2 Tbsp. water, and salt; stir to combine. Cook without stirring over medium heat until mixture turns a deep golden brown. Immediately remove from heat. Stirring constantly with a long-handled wooden spoon, very gradually add remaining 1 cup water, being careful of spatters. Mixture will clump and harden. Return pan to medium heat and stir constantly until mixture is smooth. Add espresso powder, stirring to dissolve. Add cream; cook over low heat, stirring often, until mixture begins to simmer. Remove from heat; stir in vanilla. Taste and sweeten with sugar, if desired. Pour into warm mugs. If desired, garnish with a dollop of whipped cream, topped with an orange twist. Or simply drop the orange twist into the coffee sans whipped cream.

VARIATIONS

Iced Café Crème Brûlée   After sweetening the finished drink, refrigerate until very cold, about 3 hours. Serve in tall, ice-filled glasses; top with a dollop of whipped cream, if desired.

Café Crème Brûlée Frappé (Serves 4)   Increase espresso powder to ¼ cup. Refrigerate mixture until chilled. Combine mixture with 6 scoops of slightly softened coffee, vanilla, or chocolate ice cream in a blender. Cover and process at medium speed until smooth. Pour into tall glasses; top with whipped cream, if desired. Serve with straws and iced-tea spoons.

✳ **If this is coffee, please bring me some tea; if this is tea, please bring me some coffee.**

—Abraham Lincoln, sixteenth president of the United States

Malloccino [mah-loh-CHEE-noh]

The number of marshmallows you use depends on your sweet tooth. This drink becomes very frothy, so serve it in 12-ounce mugs. *See also* Tips for Making Hot Drinks, page 184.

SERVES 2

2 cups (16 oz.) milk
12 to 16 large marshmallows
⅛ tsp. ground cinnamon
1½ Tbsp. instant espresso powder or 2 Tbsp. instant coffee granules

In a medium saucepan, combine milk, marshmallows, and cinnamon. Cook over low heat, stirring often, until marshmallows are almost melted (leave a few small lumps). Add espresso powder; stir to dissolve. Pour into warm mugs.

VARIATION

Mocha Malloccino   Add ½ cup semisweet chocolate chips with the espresso powder; stir until melted.

Cocojava

The taste of the islands in a cup. *See also* Tips for Making Hot Drinks, page 184.

SERVES 1

½ cup (4 oz.) low-fat coconut milk
½ cup (4 oz.) prepared strong coffee

toasted coconut, page 259, for garnish
(optional)

In a small saucepan, heat coconut milk and coffee together until hot. Pour into a warm mug; sprinkle with toasted coconut, if desired.

VARIATION

Chilly Cocojava The coconut milk and coffee should be chilled or at least at room temperature. Stir together in a tall glass; add ice cubes.

Café Brûlot [ka-fay broo-LOH]

In French, *brûlot* means "burnt brandy," a reference to the fact that the classic version of this drink is flamed by warming and igniting the alcohol (brandy and Cointreau) in it. This rendition is alcohol-free, so we won't, of course, be needing matches. Demitasse cups are preferred, but Irish coffee mugs or other small cups will do as well. *See also* Tips for Making Hot Drinks, page 184.

SERVES 4 TO 6

¼ cup (2 oz.) Zesty Orange Syrup, page 253, or
store-bought orange-flavored syrup, or
nonalcoholic Triple Sec
¼ cup finely julienned lemon zest
¼ cup finely julienned orange zest

1 Tbsp. packed brown sugar

1 2-inch cinnamon stick, broken in half

4 whole cloves

4 whole allspice

3 cups (24 oz.) prepared hot, strong coffee

lemon or orange twists for garnish

In a medium saucepan over medium heat, combine all ingredients except coffee and garnish. Cook, stirring occasionally, for 5 minutes. Gradually add coffee; heat just to a simmer. Ladle coffee into cups; garnish with lemon or orange twists.

✳ **Do you know how helpless you feel if you have a full cup of coffee in your hand and you start to sneeze?**

—Jean Kerr, American writer, playwright

Vanilla Suite

Coffee and vanilla have a natural affinity, but subtlety is the name of the game here, so we're using only the vanilla seeds, not the pod. I purposefully omitted dusting this drink with cocoa or cinnamon, both of which would detract from the elusive vanilla flavor. *See also* Tips for Making Hot Drinks, page 184.

SERVES 4

1½ cups (12 oz.) whole milk or half & half
1 vanilla bean, split lengthwise
3 cups (24 oz.) prepared strong coffee or 2 Tbsp.
    instant espresso powder dissolved in 3 cups
    (24 oz.) hot water
1 to 2 Tbsp. packed brown sugar (optional)

Pour milk into a medium saucepan. Using a
pointed spoon (like a grapefruit spoon) or the tip
of a pointed knife, scrape seeds from vanilla pod
into milk. Reserve pods for another use, such as
Vanilla Sugar, page 259. Over medium heat, bring milk
to a simmer. Reduce heat to low; simmer,
uncovered, for 5 minutes. Add coffee and sugar, if
desired; heat until very hot. Pour mixture into a
blender. Cover and blend until frothy, starting on low
speed and gradually increasing to high. Immediately
pour into warm mugs.

VARIATION

Frosty Vanilla Suite   After simmering milk
and vanilla, remove from heat and combine with
coffee. Sweeten with sugar, if desired. Cover and
refrigerate until chilled, about 3 hours. Pour into
blender; process at high speed until frothy. Pour
into tall glasses; top with a dollop of whipped
cream.

Café de Olla [ka-fay day OH-lah]

This rich, spicy-sweet drink from Mexico is classically made in an earthenware pot (*olla* is Spanish for "pot"). *Piloncillo* (pee-lohn-SEE-yoh) is a hard, unrefined, cone-shaped brown sugar found in Latin markets and some supermarkets. Increase or decrease the amount of *piloncillo* (or regular brown sugar), according to taste. *See also* Tips for Making Hot Drinks, page 184.

SERVES 2

2 cups (16 oz.) water
⅓ cup coarsely ground dark-roast coffee (such as Viennese)
1- to 1½-inch cinnamon stick
3 to 4 small (¾ oz.) *piloncillos,* coarsely chopped, or ¼ cup to ⅓ cup packed dark brown sugar

In a medium saucepan, combine all ingredients. Bring to a boil over medium-high heat, stirring to dissolve sugar. Reduce heat; simmer for 3 minutes. Bring to a second boil; reduce heat and simmer for another 3 minutes. Strain through a fine sieve into cups.

Mexican Mocha

The brown sugar and spices give this hot coffee–chocolate warmer its Mexican flair. *See also* Tips for Making Hot Drinks, page 184.

SERVES 4

⅓ cup instant coffee powder

⅓ cup unsweetened cocoa powder

⅔ cup packed brown sugar

¼ tsp. ground cinnamon

¼ tsp. ground allspice

⅛ tsp. ground cloves

⅛ tsp. salt

4 cups (1 qt.; 32 oz.) milk

1 Tbsp. (½ oz.) pure vanilla extract

freshly grated nutmeg for garnish

4 cinnamon sticks for garnish

Combine the first 7 ingredients in a medium saucepan. Gradually add 1 cup of the milk, stirring to combine. Stir in remaining 3 cups milk. If desired, mocha may be covered and refrigerated at this point to be heated later, or to be used for the iced variation. Just before serving, heat mocha over low heat, stirring often, until steaming hot; do not boil. Remove from heat and add vanilla; whisk until frothy. Pour into warm cups or mugs; dust with nutmeg and garnish with cinnamon sticks for stirrers.

VARIATION

Iced Mexican Mocha   Pour refrigerated mocha and vanilla into blender; process at high speed until frothy. Pour into tall, ice-filled glasses. Omit cinnamon sticks.

✳ **The smell of coffee cooking was a reason for growing up, because children were never allowed to have it and nothing haunted the nostrils all the way out to the barn as did the aroma of boiling coffee.**

—Edna Lewis, American food writer

Viennese Coffee

The whipping cream and chocolate enhance this seductive potion, which is rich enough to be two courses—coffee and dessert. *See also* Tips for Making Hot Drinks, page 184.

SERVES 8 TO 10

1½ cups (12 oz.) whipping cream, divided
8 oz. semisweet chocolate, chopped
8 cups (64 oz.) strongly prepared coffee
2 Tbsp. powdered sugar
½ cup grated chocolate for garnish

In a large, heavy saucepan, combine ¾ cup of the whipping cream and chocolate. Cook over low heat, stirring often, until chocolate is melted and mixture is smooth. Gradually stir in coffee; heat until hot. While mixture is heating, whip remaining ¾ cup whipping cream with sugar. Pour coffee into warm mugs; top with dollops of whipped cream and grated chocolate.

✳ **Coffee should be black as Hell, strong as death, and sweet as love.**

—Turkish proverb

Turkish Coffee

When made correctly, this strong, thick brew has a high concentration of caffeine, just what those who crave it are looking for. Classically it's made in a long-handled brass or copper coverless pot called an *ibrik* or a *jezve*. The coffee beans must be ground until they're as fine as flour. The creamy foam that forms on the coffee's surface is said to be a sign of good fortune; the "sludge" at the bottom should be left there. *See also* Tips for Making Hot Drinks, page 184.

MAKES 2 DEMITASSE CUPS

2 Tbsp. powdered or *extremely* finely ground
    coffee (Turkish, Mocha, Java, or Viennese
    roast)
1 cup (8 oz.) chilled water
2 tsp. sugar (optional)

In an *ibrik* or small, heavy saucepan, stir together coffee, water, and sugar, if desired; fill container only half full to prevent boil-overs. Over medium-high heat, bring mixture to a boil; do not stir. When the boiling coffee foam has reached the rim of the pot (don't let it boil over), remove from heat; stir and let stand until foam subsides. Repeat process two more times. Pour into 2 demitasse cups. Distribute coffee foam equally between servings. Let stand 2 minutes for grounds to settle.

VARIATIONS

Arabic Coffee   Use 2 tsp. sugar; add ⅛ tsp. ground cardamom.

Greek Coffee   Identical to Turkish coffee; often sweetened.

Coffee Carte

COFFEE HAS never been more popular than it is today, a fact made obvious by the proliferation of retail coffee stores and coffeehouses popping up around the United States. To some, coffee is coffee, but to others, it's an experience unto itself. I know people who consider a restaurant déclassé if it doesn't serve cappuccinos, espressos, and lattes— terms that can be intimidating to coffee neophytes. If you're new at the game, you might be interested in the following menu of coffee terms:

CAFÉ AU LAIT [ka-fay oh-LAY]
French for "coffee with milk"; equal portions of scalded milk and coffee.

CAFÉ BRÛLOT [ka-fay broo-LOH]
Coffee blended with spices, orange and lemon zests, and brandy, then flamed and served in demitasse cups.

CAFÉ LATTE [ka-fay LAH-tay]
Espresso with a liberal amount of foamy steamed milk, usually served in a tall glass mug.

CAFÉ MACCHIATO [ka-fay mah-kee-YAH-toh]
Espresso with a dollop of steamed-milk foam, served in an espresso cup.

CAFÉ MOCHA [ka-fay MOH-kah]
A café latte with chocolate added.

CAPPUCCINO [kap-poo-CHEE-noh]
Equal parts espresso, steamed milk, and milk foam, served in a regular cup or glass mug.

ESPRESSO [ehs-PREHS-soh]
A very strong brew made with dark-roasted coffee under pressure, served in a tiny espresso cup. ESPRESSO CON PANNA is an espresso with a dollop of whipped cream.

GREEK COFFEE
A rich, intensely strong boiled coffee.

IRISH COFFEE
A mélange of strong coffee, Irish whiskey, and

sugar, usually served in a glass mug with a dollop of whipped cream.

THAI COFFEE
Coffee mixed with sweetened condensed milk.

TURKISH COFFEE
An extremely strong brew made by boiling finely ground coffee, sugar, and water together.

Cold Coffee Drinks

Frappéccino [frap-peh-CHEE-noh]

Sweet and frosty—this is a perfect pick-me-up for the midafternoon blahs.

SERVES 1

⅓ cup (scant 3 oz.) *very* hot water
2 tsp. instant espresso powder
⅓ cup (scant 3 oz.) chilled water
⅓ cup (scant 3 oz.) sweetened condensed milk
4 ice cubes, coarsely crushed

Pour hot water into a blender; add coffee powder. Cover and process at medium speed until coffee is dissolved, about 15 seconds. Add chilled water, milk, and ice cubes; cover and process at high speed until mixture is smooth. Pour into a tall glass; serve with a straw.

Mochathon

If you love the marriage of coffee and chocolate, this drink's for you. For ultimate decadence, top it off with mocha or chocolate whipped cream.

SERVES 2

1½ cups (12 oz.) milk

1 rounded Tbsp. instant espresso powder

½ cup (4 oz.) Dark Chocolate Syrup, page 256, or
store-bought chocolate syrup

4 scoops coffee or chocolate ice cream, slightly softened

Mocha or Chocolate Whipped Cream, page 258,
for garnish (optional)

grated chocolate for garnish (optional)

Combine milk and espresso powder in a blender. Cover
and process at high speed until coffee dissolves. Add
chocolate syrup and ice cream; blend at medium speed
until smooth. Pour into 2 tall glasses. If desired, top
each serving with a dollop of whipped cream and
sprinkle with grated chocolate. Serve with straws.

✳ **I think if I were a woman
I'd wear coffee as a perfume.**

—John Van Druten, American playwright

Plantation Dream

Use coffee ice cubes (*see* Flavored Ice Cubes, page 261) to
give this drink an extra jolt of flavor.

SERVES 1

1 cup (8 oz.) chilled coffee
1 medium ripe banana, peeled and
  quartered
1 to 2 Tbsp. (½ to 1 oz.) cream of
  coconut

Combine all ingredients in a blender. Cover and process
at medium speed until smooth. Pour into a tall glass; add
ice cubes. Serve with a straw.

Affogatto [ah-foh-GAH-toh]

This simple concoction, whose name comes from the Italian *affogare* ("to drown"), combines the coffee and dessert courses, creating an exceedingly satisfying "espresso sundae."

SERVES 1

1 heaping tsp. espresso powder
⅓ cup (scant 3 oz.) boiling water
1 scoop vanilla gelato or ice cream, slightly
  softened
lemon twist for garnish (optional)

Dissolve espresso powder in boiling water. Place gelato
in a small cup or sherbet glass; slowly add hot espresso.
If desired, garnish with lemon twist.

✳ **Moderation is a fatal thing. . . .**
Nothing succeeds like excess.

So said Anglo-Irish playwright Oscar Wilde, who was known for his tongue-in-cheek humor. But this inimitable wit's philosophy was dead wrong in the case of the great French writer Honoré de Balzac, who purportedly died from caffeine poisoning because he consumed fifty-plus cups of coffee a day. But then, perhaps Balzac wouldn't have written so brilliantly if he'd been drinking tea.

Coffee with a Kiss

The "kiss" is a soupçon of sweetness from flavored syrup, of which there are myriad flavors, including hazelnut, English toffee, and butter rum (*see* Syrups, Flavored, page 34).

SERVES 1

1 cup (8 oz.) prepared strong coffee, preferably chilled

1 Tbsp. (½ oz.) flavored syrup, store-bought or homemade, pages 251–256

whipped cream for garnish (optional)

Combine coffee and syrup in a tall glass; stir to combine. Add ice cubes; garnish with whipped cream, if desired.

Orange Oasis

The combination of coffee, chocolate, and orange is seductive, whether enjoyed cold or hot.

SERVES 1

1 cup (8 oz.) prepared strong coffee, preferably
chilled

1 Tbsp. (½ oz.) Dark Chocolate Syrup, page 256,
or store-bought chocolate syrup

1 Tbsp. (½ oz.) thawed frozen orange juice concentrate
superfine sugar or Sugar Syrup, page 251
(optional)
orange slice for garnish

In a tall glass, stir together the first 3 ingredients. Sweeten with sugar or sugar syrup, if desired. Add ice cubes; garnish with orange slice.

VARIATION

Torrid Orange Oasis   Heat coffee, chocolate syrup, juice concentrate, and sugar until very hot. Pour into a warm mug. Top with a dollop of whipped cream and orange twist.

Café Shakerato

An iced coffee "cocktail" from Italy. If you don't have a cocktail shaker, a blender can do the job (coarsely crush ice cubes before adding them to the blender). Either way, you want to "shake" the dickens out of the ingredients so the resulting drink has a foamy cap.

SERVES 1

⅓ cup (scant 3 oz.) prepared hot espresso or 1 tsp.
espresso coffee powder dissolved in ⅓ cup
(scant 3 oz.) hot water
superfine sugar or Sugar Syrup, page 251
(optional)
4 ice cubes

Combine coffee, sugar, and ice cubes in a shaker or blender jar. Cover and shake or blend at high speed until ice cubes are almost dissolved and mixture is foamy. Pour into chilled champagne flute or medium wineglass. If using shaker, remove strainer before pouring so remaining ice goes into glass.

VARIATION

Cappuccino Shakerato   Add 1 to 2 Tbsp. (½ to 1 oz.) milk or half & half before shaking. Pour into wineglass; dust with cocoa powder or ground cinnamon.

Eight

Tea Drinks

I F YOU'RE AS passionate about tea as the Reverend Sydney Smith, you'll love this chapter, which includes some old recipe favorites as well as many new creations. But as with all things in life, such drinks need a good foundation, namely a nicely brewed tea. Here are a few tips and techniques to help make your brew turn out perfectly every time.

Tea Tips

✳ Store tea, tightly sealed, in a cool, dark place for up to 1 year.

✳ Personalize tea bags or loose tea by storing them in an airtight jar with cinnamon sticks or other spices, citrus peels, or vanilla beans.

✳ When making tea, always begin with fresh, cold water; bring it to a boil. Count on 6 ounces of water per cup of tea.

✳ Use 1 heaping teaspoon of loose tea or 1 tea bag per cup. Put loose leaves in a tea caddy (also called an "infuser") to avoid straining.

✳ Use a china, glass, or ceramic teapot—metal can affect the tea's flavor.

✳ Warm a teapot before beginning the steeping process by filling it with boiling water; let the water stand a few minutes before discarding.

✳ Put the tea caddy or tea bags in the warmed teapot, add freshly boiled water, and stir. Replace the teapot lid, cover with a tea cozy, and let steep 4 to 6 minutes, depending on the tea and your palate.

✳ While the tea is steeping, warm the cup(s) by filling them with hot water.

❋ Remove the tea caddy or tea bags; give the tea a gentle stir. If using loose tea without a caddy, strain into a cup.

❋ If using milk in the tea, use whole milk, which has the perfect textural balance for tea. Skim milk or cream won't make the same magic.

Hot Tea Drinks

Almond Tea Latte

This is pure comfort delivered with a double dose of almond flavor. *See also* Tips for Making Hot Drinks, page 184.

SERVES 4

2 cups (16 oz.) water
4 almond-flavored tea bags
1½ cups (12 oz.) milk
1½ Tbsp. (¾ oz.) orgeat syrup or other almond-
    flavored syrup
ground allspice for garnish

In a medium saucepan, bring water to a boil; remove from heat. Add tea bags; cover and steep 5 minutes. Remove tea bags, squeezing to extract as much liquid as possible. Stir in milk and almond-flavored syrup; bring to a simmer. Pour into warm cups; sprinkle with allspice.

VARIATIONS

Spiced Almond Tea Latte   Add ½ tsp. each ground allspice and cinnamon with the milk and almond syrup.

Iced Almond Tea Latte   Prepare tea; refrigerate until chilled. In a medium pitcher, stir together tea, milk, and syrup. Divide between 4 tall, ice-filled glasses; sprinkle with allspice.

✱ **You can taste and feel, but not describe, the exquisite state of repose produced by tea, that precious drink which drives away the five causes of sorrow.**
—Emperor Ch'ien Lung, Chinese emperor

Chai Tea

For centuries this aromatic spiced tea has been a favorite in India, where *chaiwallahs* (vendors) tend chai stalls, which are popular gathering places. There are a variety of packaged chai teas (also called *masala chai*), including liquid concentrates, powder, and loose-leaf tea with spices. They are available in Indian markets, natural food stores, and specialty tea and coffee shops. You'll also find a bevy of bottled, variously flavored chai teas, most of which are too sweet for my palate. I like this homemade version, which can be as sweet or not as you like. *See also* Tips for Making Hot Drinks, page 184.

SERVES 4 TO 6

4 cups (32 oz.) water
8 cardamom pods

6 whole cloves

2 Tbsp. chopped, peeled ginger

1 cinnamon stick

½ tsp. whole coriander seeds

½ tsp. black peppercorns

1 heaping Tbsp. loose black tea, preferably
Darjeeling

1 cup (8 oz.) milk

sugar (optional)

In a medium saucepan, combine water, cardamom, cloves, ginger, cinnamon, coriander, and peppercorns. Bring to a boil over high heat; stir in tea leaves. Reduce heat to low; cover and simmer for 10 minutes. Add milk and, if desired, sweeten with sugar. Bring tea back to a simmer, stirring once or twice. Strain into warm cups.

VARIATION

Iced Chai Tea　Refrigerate strained tea mixture for at least 4 hours. Pour into tall glasses filled halfway with ice cubes; garnish with slices of crystallized ginger.

Cranberry Comfort

See also Tips for Making Hot Drinks, page 184.

SERVES 4

2 cups (16 oz.) cranberry juice

6 whole cloves

½ cinnamon stick

4 cranberry-flavored tea bags

2 cups (16 oz.) fresh orange juice

4 orange twists for garnish

In a medium saucepan, combine cranberry juice, cloves, and cinnamon stick; bring to a boil. Add tea bags; cover and steep 6 minutes. Remove tea bags, squeezing to . extract as much liquid as possible. Add orange juice; heat just until mixture is very hot. Strain into warm cups; drop an orange twist into each serving.

Ginger-Maple Medley

There's something about this spicy, maple-scented brew that makes me yearn for a cold day just so I can serve it. *See also* Tips for Making Hot Drinks, page 184.

SERVES 4

4 cups (32 oz.) water

½ tsp. ground ginger

½ tsp. ground cinnamon

6 ginger-flavored tea bags

3 Tbsp. (1½ oz.) pure maple syrup

⅓ cup (ample 2½ oz.) whipping cream (optional)

In a medium saucepan, bring water, ginger, and cinnamon to a boil; remove from heat. Add tea bags; cover and steep 5 minutes. Remove tea bags, squeezing to extract as much liquid as possible. Add maple syrup and, if desired, cream. Bring tea to a simmer, stirring to dissolve syrup. Pour into warm cups.

Taking Care of Teapots and Kettles

✳ To avoid teapot stains, remove the tea from the pot as soon as you're finished.

✳ Remove teapot stains by rubbing them with a paste of baking soda and water; wash well with soap and hot water.

✳ To cure a stale-smelling teapot, put in 2 teaspoons of baking soda and fill with boiling water. Cover and let stand until cool. Wash as usual with soap and water.

✳ Remove lime deposits from a tea kettle by filling it with equal amounts of white vinegar and water. Bring to a boil; let stand overnight. The next morning, wash well with soap and water.

Apple Smack Tea

For a less sweet tea, use 2 cups apple juice and 2 cups water. *See also* Tips for Making Hot Drinks, page 184.

SERVES 4

4 cups (32 oz.) apple juice

8 whole cloves
8 whole allspice
2 cinnamon sticks
5 black tea bags

In a medium saucepan, combine apple juice and spices; bring to a boil. Reduce heat and simmer for 5 minutes. Remove from heat; add tea bags, stirring well. Cover and steep 5 minutes. Use a slotted spoon to remove tea bags and spices, pressing down on tea bags to remove as much liquid as possible. Pour into warm cups.

VARIATION

Apple Cream Tea After removing tea bags and spices from steeped tea, stir in ½ cup (4 oz.) half & half or whipping cream. Heat over low heat until simmering.

✳ **Love and scandal are the best sweeteners of tea.**
—Henry Fielding, English novelist

Iced Teas

Dᴵᴰ ʏᴼᵁ know that Americans were the first to drink tea iced? Many pundits claim that iced tea was invented at the 1904 St. Louis International Exposition when tea plantation owner Richard Blechynden added ice to his hot tea to lure wilting attendees to his booth. But as with so many things, it ain't necessarily so. For you see, in his 1860 book *How to Live, New York Tribune* writer Solon Robinson wrote: "Last summer we got in the habit of taking the tea iced, and really thought it better than hot." To those of us who relish iced tea's refreshing salvation on a sweltering day, it matters not a whit when iced tea was first invented, but simply that it *was*.

Grape Escape

For a special presentation, make white grape juice ice cubes (*see* Flavored Ice Cubes, page 261) the day before you serve the tea.

SERVES 2

1 cup (8 oz.) chilled prepared green tea
1 cup (8 oz.) chilled white grape juice
2 mint sprigs (optional)

Combine tea and juice; divide evenly between 2 tall glasses. Add ice cubes; garnish with mint sprigs, if desired.

Tips for Making Iced Tea

✳ Use approximately twice as much tea when brewing tea that will be iced.

✳ For clear iced tea, combine tea leaves or bags with cold water; cover and refrigerate for at least 24 hours. Strain the tea as you pour it into the glasses.

✳ *Sun tea,* also a clear brew, is made by combining tea leaves or tea bags and water in a clear pitcher or jar. Cover and let stand in the sun for 4 hours before straining and chilling.

✳ Tea will become cloudy if made with boiling water and refrigerated while hot. To clear cloudy tea, stir in a little boiling water.

✳ Hot-brewed tea will stay clear if allowed to cool to room temperature before being refrigerated.

✳ **A woman is like a tea bag—only in hot water do you realize how strong she is.**

—Nancy Reagan, American First Lady, actress, author

Frost-Tea Cooler

Substitute orange sherbet for the ice cream for a double orange whammy.

SERVES 6

2 cups (16 oz.) water
¼ tsp. ground cinnamon
¼ tsp. ground allspice
⅛ tsp. ground cloves
6 black currant tea bags
1 cup (8 oz.) chilled milk
1 6-oz. can frozen orange juice concentrate
1 pint vanilla ice cream, slightly softened
6 orange slices

In a small saucepan, combine water and spices; bring to a boil. Remove from heat; add tea bags. Cover and let steep 5 minutes. Strain into a blender, pressing tea bags to extract as much liquid as possible. Refrigerate, uncovered, for 2 hours (or freeze 1 hour), or until cold. May be covered and refrigerated overnight. When ready to serve, add milk and orange juice concentrate to tea in blender; process at medium speed until combined. Spoon in half the ice cream; process until smooth. Divide remaining ice cream evenly between 6 tall glasses; pour in tea mixture. Garnish each serving with an orange slice.

Georgian Comfort

Substitute mango, guava, or passion fruit nectar for a tropical twist.

SERVES 1

½ cup (4 oz.) chilled prepared spice-flavored tea
½ cup (4 oz.) peach nectar
1 Tbsp. (½ oz.) fresh lemon juice
chilled seltzer water or club soda
lemon twist

In a tall glass, combine tea, peach nectar, and lemon juice. Add 3 to 4 ice cubes. Top with seltzer; drop in twist.

Teazazz

SERVES 8

8 cups (64 oz.) water
2 Tbsp. minced, peeled ginger
1 tsp. ground cinnamon
1 6-oz. can frozen raspberry-cranberry juice
    concentrate
10 Celestial Seasonings Red Zinger tea bags
superfine sugar
8 slices crystallized ginger

In a large saucepan, stir together water, ginger, cinnamon, and juice concentrate; bring to a boil. Reduce heat to low; cover and simmer for 10 minutes. Bring mixture back to a boil. Remove from heat and add tea bags; cover and steep 6 minutes. Strain into pitcher, pressing down on tea bags to remove as much liquid as possible. Refrigerate until chilled, about 4 hours. Sweeten to taste with sugar. Pour into wineglasses filled halfway with ice cubes; garnish with crystallized ginger slices.

VARIATION

Hot Teazazz After straining, return tea to pan; sweeten to taste with sugar. Bring to a simmer. Serve in teacups with ginger-slice garnish. *See also* Tips for Making Hot Drinks, page 184.

Tea Terminology

A LTHOUGH ALL tea plants belong to the same species, varying climates, soils, and processing techniques combine to create a multitude of distinctive tea leaves. Here's a breakdown of the basic types:

BLACK TEA
Leaves that have been fermented before being heated and dried, the result of which is a dark, reddish-brown brew. Black teas—which include

Darjeeling, English Breakfast, and Lapsang Souchong—have more assertive flavors than green or oolong teas. The term "orange pekoe" refers not to a flavor or color, but to a black tea leaf's size, which is smaller than that of the medium pekoe leaf.

GREEN TEA
Unfermented, steamed, and dried leaves that produce a greenish-yellow, slightly bitter tea. Two of the more well-known green teas are Gunpowder and Tencha.

OOLONG TEA,
Leaves that have been partially fermented, which produces a flavor, a color, and an aroma somewhere between those of black and green teas. The best known oolong is Taiwan's Formosa Oolong.

HERB TEA (also called *tisane*)
This isn't a true tea because it isn't based on tea-plant leaves but, rather, on various herbs, flowers, and spices.

✳ It is the destiny of mint to be crushed.
—Waverly Root, American writer

Mint Julep Tea

The classic mint julep (based on bourbon) is the official drink of the Kentucky Derby, run on the first Saturday in May. This invigorating tea-based tonic can be enjoyed as soon as there's mint to be picked.

SERVES 6

2 cups loosely packed fresh mint leaves

⅓ cup sugar

2 Tbsp. (1 oz.) water

8 green tea bags

6 cups (48 oz.) boiling water

5 cups crushed ice

6 mint sprigs for garnish

In a large, heatproof bowl, muddle mint leaves, sugar, and 2 Tbsp. water until mint leaves are crushed. Add tea and boiling water; cover and steep 6 minutes. Strain tea, pressing down on tea bags to remove as much liquid as possible. Cover and refrigerate strained tea until very cold, 2 to 4 hours. Divide crushed ice between 6 tall glasses. Fill with tea; garnish with mint sprigs.

VARIATION

Hot Mint Julep Tea   After steeping and straining tea, pour into warm cups; garnish with mint sprigs. *See also* Tips for Making Hot Drinks, page 184.

Yogurtea

Use your favorite flavor of tea and yogurt. I love orange-spice tea with apricot-mango or orange yogurt.

SERVES 2

1½ cups (12 oz.) chilled prepared tea
¾ to 1 cup (6 to 8 oz.) flavored yogurt

Combine tea and yogurt in a blender. Cover and process at medium speed until smooth. Pour into tall, ice-filled glasses.

Orangeburst Tea

SERVES 4

4 cups (32 oz.) fresh orange juice
5 black currant tea bags
3 Tbsp. (1½ oz.) fresh lemon juice
1 cinnamon stick
superfine sugar (optional)
4 orange slices for garnish

In a pitcher combine orange juice, tea bags, lemon juice, and cinnamon stick. Cover and refrigerate overnight or at least 8 hours. Remove tea bags and cinnamon stick, pressing down on tea bags to remove as much liquid as possible. Sweeten to taste with sugar, if desired. Pour into tall glasses filled halfway with ice cubes; garnish with orange slices.

Bubble Tea

IF YOU like something to chew on with your beverage, you're going to love bubble tea. Now wildly popular around the world, bubble tea originated in Taiwan during the early 1980s. Also called *pearl tea, boba tea, tapioca milk tea, tapioca ball drink, bobo nai has,* and *zhen shou nai cha,* this unique concoction began as flavor-infused tea shaken with ice (which causes bubbles) and poured into a glass at the bottom of which rest more "bubbles" in the form of big, black tapioca pearls. Today the term "bubble drink" refers to almost any drink with tapioca pearls bobbing at the bottom served with fat straws big enough to suck up the pearls along with the liquid (*see* Fresh Fruit Bubble Drink, page 115).

The tapioca used in bubble drinks isn't your mama's tapioca. We're talking big black orbs, twice the size of regular pearl tapioca, with a soft, chewing gum/Jell-O consistency. And whereas regular tapioca is made from cassava root, most of the tapioca used for bubble tea is sweet-potato-based and colored with caramel. During cooking, the light brown pearls

turn almost black, making for a showy presentation. Although some Asian markets carry jars of cooked tapioca pearls in syrup, they're hard to find. I finally located the large uncooked pearls (which are about 5/16 inch in diameter uncooked and half again as large cooked) through the Internet at Bubble Tea Supply (808-951-7883 or www.bubbleteasupply.com). The company sells everything necessary for making bubble drinks, including the fat straws and myriad powdered flavorings, from honeydew to coconut to taro (the most popular, I'm told).

Tapioca Pearls (for bubble drinks)

MAKES ABOUT 2⅓ CUPS
(enough tapioca pearls for 7 drinks)

about 1½ cups (12 oz.) Sugar Syrup, page 251
7½ cups (60 oz.) water
1½ cups tapioca pearls (about 5/16 inch in diameter)
¼ tsp. pure almond extract (optional)

Prepare sugar syrup; set aside to cool. In a large pot, bring water to a boil. Add tapioca, stirring to loosen any pearls that stick to the bottom of the pan—the pearls will rise to the surface. Return to a boil, then reduce heat to between medium and medium-low, just enough heat so the liquid maintains a slow boil. Cover and cook for 45 minutes.

Remove from heat; let stand, covered, for 30 minutes. Pour tapioca pearls into a colander. Rinse well with lukewarm water to remove any excess starch, tossing the pearls as you rinse. Drain pearls well; turn into a container with a cover. Add 1 to 1½ cups sugar syrup, enough to cover the pearls. If desired, stir in almond extract. Cover and refrigerate for up to a week. Use a slotted spoon to transfer pearls from sugar syrup to glass. If pearls have become too chewy, cover with hot water and microwave for 30 seconds. Or pour boiling water over pearls and let stand 30 seconds. Sugar syrup may be covered, refrigerated, and reused for your next batch of tapioca pearls.

Bubble Tea

You can flavor bubble teas with various syrups or powdered flavorings (*see* www.bubbleteasupply.com).

SERVES 1

⅓ cup cooked tapioca pearls
1¼ cups (10 oz.) strongly prepared black, oolong, green, or chai tea
8 ice cubes, coarsely crushed
Sugar Syrup, page 251, flavored syrup, or superfine sugar to taste

Spoon tapioca pearls into a large, tall glass. In a cocktail shaker or blender, combine remaining ingredients. Shake

vigorously or blend at high speed until mixture is frothy.
Pour into glass over pearls; serve with a fat straw.

VARIATIONS

Bubble Milk Tea   Add ⅓ cup (scant 3 oz.) milk or half
& half before shaking.

Bubble Iced Coffee   Substitute strongly brewed
coffee for the tea.

Spiced Cream Tea

Use any spiced tea (such as Constant Comment) for this
tea ice cream "soda." Make it well ahead of time so the tea
is good and cold.

SERVES 1

1 to 2 scoops vanilla ice cream, slightly softened
about 1 cup (8 oz.) chilled prepared orange-spice
    tea
orange slice for garnish

Scoop ice cream into a tall glass. Top with tea; garnish with
orange slice. Serve with a straw and an iced-tea spoon.

Thai Iced Tea

A rendition of the spicy-sweet tea found in all Thai restaurants. Thai tea is flavored with star anise and can be found

in tea and specialty gourmet shops, Asian markets, and the ethnic food section of many supermarkets. Orange pekoe or Lapsang Souchong can be substituted. You can also omit the half & half and sugar and substitute about 1¼ cups sweetened condensed milk.

SERVES 6

6 cups (48 oz.) water
8 Thai tea bags
⅓ cup packed brown sugar
2 tsp. ground cinnamon
1 cup (8 oz.) half & half or evaporated milk
about 5 cups crushed ice
6 mint sprigs for garnish

In a medium saucepan, combine water, tea bags, sugar, and cinnamon; bring to a boil. Remove from heat; cover and steep 1 hour. Squeeze as much liquid as possible from tea bags. Pour tea into pitcher; stir in half & half. Refrigerate until chilled. To serve, fill each glass two-thirds full with crushed ice. Pour in tea; garnish with mint sprig.

✳ **Iced tea is too pure and natural a creation not to have been invented as soon as tea, ice, and hot weather crossed paths.**

—John Egerton, American author

Blueberry Tease

A kiss of maple syrup adds magic to this frosty cooler. If fresh blueberries aren't in season, use partially thawed dry-pack frozen blueberries.

SERVES 4

3 cups fresh blueberries
1½ cups (12 oz.) chilled, strongly prepared orange-spice tea
2 Tbsp. (1 oz.) pure maple syrup
½ tsp. ground cinnamon
¼ tsp. freshly grated nutmeg
2 scoops vanilla or orange ice cream, slightly softened
freshly grated nutmeg for garnish

Combine blueberries, tea, syrup, and spices in a blender. Cover and process at high speed until smooth. Add ice cream; process at medium speed until smooth. Pour into tall glasses; sprinkle with nutmeg. Serve with straws.

Cranberry Swizzle

The flavors of cranberry, raspberry, and orange combine to make a sensationally tangy-sweet tea.

SERVES 10

8 cups (64 oz.) chilled, strongly prepared cranberry or orange-spice tea

2 cups (16 oz.) fresh orange juice
1 6-oz. can frozen cranberry-raspberry juice
   concentrate
superfine sugar
10 orange slices for garnish

Combine the first 3 ingredients in a large pitcher; sweeten to taste with sugar. Cover and refrigerate until chilled, about 2 hours. Serve in tall, ice-filled glasses; garnish with orange slices.

Lemonade Iced Tea

Tea and lemonade lovers alike will love this bodacious blend. I've used a variety of tea flavors, from cranberry to black currant to orange-spice, with delicious results. For a pretty-in-pink look, try pink lemonade concentrate. Because cold temperatures mute flavors, don't sweeten this drink until it's chilled.

SERVES 10

8 cups (64 oz.) water
10 tea bags
1 12-oz. can frozen lemonade concentrate
Sugar Syrup (page 251) or superfine sugar
   (optional)
lemon slices or mint sprigs for garnish
   (optional)

In a medium saucepan, bring 4 cups of the water to a boil. Remove from heat; stir in tea bags. Cover and steep 6 minutes. Use a slotted spoon to remove tea bags, pressing down to remove as much liquid as possible. Add remaining 4 cups water and frozen concentrate, stirring to combine. Cover and refrigerate until very cold. Sweeten to taste with sugar syrup or sugar, if desired, stirring well to combine. Pour into tall, ice-filled glasses; garnish with lemon slices or mint sprigs, if desired.

Nine

Hot Drinks

NOTHING'S MORE soothing when the weather's frosty than warming one's hands on a toasty mug and slowly sipping its contents. Of course, one of the all-time favorite warmers is hot chocolate, perfect for chasing winter's chill as well as soothing the soul. Here you'll find potions ranging in flavor from ultrachocolaty, to mint- or orange-spiked chocolate, to white chocolate. On days when you're not in the mood for chocolate (personally, I've never had such a day), the simple satisfaction of Cinnamon-Honey Heater, Sugar-Bush Hummer, or Candied Apple Cider (just to name a few) are here for your enjoyment. So name your pleasure and step up to the bar for some hot drinks that are guaranteed to warm the cockles of your heart.

Tips for Making Hot Drinks

Serve hot drinks only in heatproof (tempered) glasses, cups, or punch bowls. Be careful if the hot drinks are served in metal cups or mugs—metal holds heat so well it can easily burn your lips. Preheat nonmetal glasses, cups, or bowls by filling them with very hot water and letting them stand for about 3 minutes. To help disseminate the heat of the drink and to keep the container from cracking, place a metal spoon in the cup or glass (or a metal ladle in a punch bowl) and slowly pour the hot drink onto it.

Chocolate Thunder

Someone once said, "Chocolate is a passionate, sensuous connection to all my hedonistic yearnings." Okay, it was me. But I can't help myself when it comes to chocolate, and this hot drinkable version is one of my favorites. If you really want to get naughty, top it off with chocolate-flavored whipped cream or a scoop of chocolate ice cream, both of which melt seductively into the hot chocolate. *See also* Tips for Making Hot Drinks, above.

SERVES 4

2 cups (16 oz.) whipping cream
2 cups (16 oz.) half & half or milk
¼ tsp. salt
12 oz. semisweet chocolate chips
2 tsp. pure vanilla extract
Chocolate Whipped Cream (page 258)
  or chocolate ice cream for garnish
  (optional)

In a large saucepan, combine cream, half & half, and
salt; bring to a simmer over medium heat. Add
chocolate chips; stir until melted and mixture is smooth.
Remove from heat and add vanilla; whisk until frothy.
Pour into warm mugs. If desired, top with a dollop of
whipped cream or a scoop of ice cream.

✳ **After having chocolate you feel godlike, as
though you can conquer enemies, lead armies,
entice lovers.**
—Emily Luchetti, American chef, author

Hot Orange Chocolate

Chocolate-covered candied orange peel makes a lovely
garnish for this drink and can be found in candy stores

and many supermarkets. *See also* Tips for Making Hot Drinks, page 184.

SERVES 4

> 4 cups (32 oz.) half & half (or equal parts milk and
>   half & half)
> 12 oz. semisweet chocolate, coarsely chopped
> zest of 1 large orange, cut into large pieces
> ¼ tsp. freshly grated nutmeg
> ½ cup (4 oz.) whipping cream, whipped
>   (optional)
> chocolate-dipped candied orange peel
>   (optional)

Combine half & half, chocolate, orange zest, and nutmeg in a large saucepan. Bring to a simmer over medium heat. Reduce heat to low; cook for 10 minutes, stirring often, until chocolate has melted and mixture is smooth. Use a slotted spoon to remove and discard orange zest. Pour into warm mugs. If desired, garnish each serving with a dollop of whipped cream and chocolate-covered candied orange peel.

French Mint

This drink reminds me of thin, dark chocolate-covered mints with a creamy, smooth filling. Decadent! *See also* Tips for Making Hot Drinks, page 184.

SERVES 4

⅓ cup unsweetened cocoa powder
⅔ cup sugar
¼ tsp. salt
4 cups (32 oz.) whipping cream
1 tsp. peppermint extract
½ tsp. pure vanilla extract
whipped cream for garnish (optional)
crushed hard peppermint candy for garnish
   (optional)
peppermint stick candy for stirrer
   (optional)

In a medium saucepan, stir together cocoa powder, sugar, and salt. Gradually stir in cream. Cook over medium heat, stirring constantly, until mixture begins to simmer. Remove from heat; stir in peppermint and vanilla extracts. Pour into warmed mugs. If desired, top with a dollop of whipped cream sprinkled with crushed candy; add peppermint candy stirrer.

✳ **There's no metaphysics on earth like chocolate.**
—Fernando Pessoa, Portuguese poet

Mexican Hot Chocolate

Using a blender is a quick but unconventional way to froth this drink. Traditional cooks use the Mexican *molinillo*, a special chocolate beater for which a whisk may be substituted. *See also* Tips for Making Hot Drinks, page 184.

SERVES 4

4 cups (32 oz.) milk or water
1 (3.3 oz.) tablet Mexican chocolate, coarsely chopped
1 Tbsp. finely chopped Mexican chocolate for garnish (optional)

In a medium saucepan, combine milk and chocolate tablet. Bring to a simmer over medium-low heat. Cook for 3 minutes, stirring often. Turn into a blender. Cover and process at low speed, gradually increasing to high speed. Pour immediately into warm mugs; sprinkle with chopped Mexican chocolate, if desired.

Hot White Chocolate

White chocolate isn't true chocolate because it contains no chocolate liquor and, likewise, very little "chocolate" flavor. Instead, it's usually a mixture of sugar, cocoa butter, milk solids, lecithin, and vanilla. But ask white chocolate lovers if they care, and the answer will be a resounding "no!" Try this drink and you may become a convert. *See also* Tips for Making Hot Drinks, page 184.

SERVES 2

2½ cups (20 oz.) half & half
¾ cup white chocolate chips or white chocolate,
    coarsely chopped
¼ tsp. salt
¼ tsp. pure vanilla extract
whipped cream for garnish (optional)

In a medium saucepan, combine half & half, white chocolate, and salt. Cook over medium-low heat, stirring continually, until mixture is smooth. Remove from heat and add vanilla; whisk until frothy. Pour into warm mugs. If desired, garnish with a dollop of whipped cream.

Raspberry Cocoa

I love the combination of raspberries and chocolate, but you can create your own magic with another flavored syrup—hazelnut, perhaps? In which case, this drink becomes Hazelnut Cocoa. *See also* Tips for Making Hot Drinks, page 184.

SERVES 2

2 Tbsp. unsweetened cocoa powder
½ cup (4 oz.) raspberry-flavored syrup

2 cups (16 oz.) milk or half & half
whipped cream for garnish (optional)

Spoon cocoa powder into a medium saucepan. Gradually add syrup, stirring until smooth. Stir in milk. Bring to a simmer over medium-low heat, stirring often. Pour into warm mugs. If desired, top each serving with a dollop of whipped cream.

S'More Sipper

It's a deprived child who's never tasted a s'more, a toasted marshmallow and chocolate square sandwiched between two graham crackers, which tastes so good (at least to children) one always wants "some more." Here we have a s'more in a mug, sans graham crackers. For a less sweet potable, try the Mocha S'More Sipper variation. *See also* Tips for Making Hot Drinks, page 184.

SERVES 2

3 Tbsp. unsweetened cocoa powder
1 Tbsp. sugar
⅛ tsp. salt
2 cups (16 oz.) milk
½ cup marshmallow fluff
(or *crème*)

In a small saucepan, combine cocoa powder, sugar, salt, and ½ cup of the milk; stir until combined. Stir in remaining milk; cook over low heat, stirring occasionally, until mixture comes to a simmer. Meanwhile, spoon ¼ cup marshmallow fluff into each of 2 warm mugs. Add hot cocoa, stirring to loosen marshmallow from bottom. Serve immediately with spoons. Sip the cocoa through the marshmallow cap or stir the marshmallow into the cocoa until it melts.

VARIATION

Mocha S'More Sipper   Add 1 to 1½ tsp. instant espresso powder to milk mixture before heating.

✳ Half past nine—high time for supper;
"Cocoa, love?" "Of course, my dear."
Helen thinks it quite delicious,
John prefers it now to beer.
Knocking back the sepia potion,
Hubby winks, says, "Who's for bed?"
"Shan't be long," says Helen softly,
Cheeks a faintly flushing red.
For they've tumbled on the secret
Of a love that never wanes,
Rapt beneath the tumbled bedclothes,
Cocoa coursing through their veins.
—Stanley J. Sharpless, American poet

Glühwein [GLEW-vine]

Glühwein is German for "glow wine" and gets its name from the fact that it "glows" with heat. *See also* Tips for Making Hot Drinks, page 184.

SERVES 1

1 cup (8 oz.) dealcoholized red wine
1 tsp. sugar or honey
2 whole cloves
1 2-inch strip orange peel
1 2-inch strip lemon peel
½ cinnamon stick

In a small saucepan, combine all ingredients; heat until simmering. Pour into a warm mug.

Cinnamon Toast Toddy

Calorie watchers can omit the butter and this drink will be almost as good—I said *almost!* *See also* Tips for Making Hot Drinks, page 184.

SERVES 1

1 cup (8 oz.) milk
½ to 1 Tbsp. packed brown sugar
¼ tsp. ground cinnamon
¼-inch-thick pat unsalted butter
ground cinnamon for garnish

In a small saucepan, combine first 3 ingredients; heat until simmering. Pour into a warm mug. Float butter on top; sprinkle with more ground cinnamon.

VARIATION

Chocolate–Cinnamon Toast Toddy   Add 1 Tbsp. unsweetened cocoa powder and increase sugar to 2 Tbsp.

✳ **In Bali, women are forbidden to touch coconut palms lest the fertility of the tree be drained off into the woman, apparently considered less important.**
—Waverly Root, American writer

Macaroon Hottie

In this drink the spicy-coconut fragrance alone is enough to soothe the most savage day. *See also* Tips for Making Hot Drinks, page 184.

SERVES 2

2½ cups (20 oz.) low-fat coconut milk

2 Tbsp. sugar

½ cinnamon stick

4 whole cloves

4 whole peppercorns
toasted coconut, page 259, for garnish (optional)

In a small saucepan over medium-high heat, bring all
ingredients except garnish to a boil. Reduce heat; cover
and simmer for 10 minutes. Strain through a sieve
into warm mugs. If desired, sprinkle with toasted
coconut.

Hot Fluffernutter

A drink inspired by the original fluffernutter, a sandwich
created in 1961 by Durkee-Mower, Inc., to promote their
Marshmallow Fluff. In this sandwich, Marshmallow Fluff
is spread on one slice of bread, peanut butter on the other.
If you think that sounds good, you're going to love this
fluffernutter in a mug. *See also* Tips for Making Hot
Drinks, page 184.

SERVES 1

1 cup (8 oz.) very hot milk
⅓ cup marshmallow fluff (also called "creme")
3 Tbsp. creamy peanut butter
pinch of cinnamon

Combine all ingredients in a blender. Cover and begin
blending at the lowest speed, gradually increasing to
high speed, until smooth. Pour into a large, warm mug.

Sugar-Bush Hummer

A grove of maple trees is called a "sugar bush," and maple-tapping season finds workers inserting spouts into the trees from which they hang buckets to catch the sap. The sap is boiled until much of the water has evaporated, leaving the silky syrup we all know and love. Look for pure maple syrup, which delivers a delicate, clean taste— "maple flavored syrup" is little more than flavored corn syrup. *See also* Tips for Making Hot Drinks, page 184.

SERVES 1

1 cup (8 oz.) milk
2 to 3 Tbsp. (1 to 1½ oz.) pure maple syrup
pinch of freshly grated nutmeg
pinch of ground cinnamon
¼ tsp. pure vanilla extract

In a small saucepan over medium-low heat, combine milk, syrup, and spices; heat until simmering. Pour into a warm mug; stir in vanilla.

Cinnamon-Honey Heater

My grandmother swore this brew relieved her arthritis. It's also an incredibly inviting quaff on cold winter days. Grandma used honey, but I love the taste of maple in this drink. *See also* Tips for Making Hot Drinks, page 184.

SERVES 1

1 Tbsp. (½ oz.) pure maple syrup or honey
1 to 2 tsp. fresh lemon juice
½ tsp. ground cinnamon
½ tsp. ground ginger
about 1 cup (8 oz.) boiling water

Combine maple syrup, lemon juice, and spices in a warm mug. Slowly add boiling water, stirring until maple syrup dissolves.

 The only way to get rid of a temptation is to yield to it.

—Oscar Wilde, Anglo-Irish playwright, critic

Tropical Heat Wave

An exotic flavor combination that evokes thoughts of tropical islands. *See also* Tips for Making Hot Drinks, page 184.

SERVES 2

2 cups (16 oz.) half & half or milk
½ cup (4 oz.) frozen pineapple juice concentrate
⅓ cup (scant 3 oz.) cream of coconut
¼ tsp. almond extract
toasted coconut, page 259, for garnish (optional)

In a medium saucepan, combine half & half, juice concentrate, and cream of coconut. Cook over medium-low heat, stirring often, until mixture begins to simmer. Remove from heat; stir in almond extract. Pour into warm mugs. If desired, sprinkle with toasted coconut.

✳ **If I think I'm about to get a cold and feel achy and chilled, I know it's time for hot apple cider....**

—Joyce Goldstein, American restaurateur, author

Candied Apple Cider

Red cinnamon candies give this cider its snap. The flavor reminds me of those bright red candied apples I used to love as a kid. *See also* Tips for Making Hot Drinks, page 184.

SERVES 4

4 cups (32 oz.) apple cider
½ cup red cinnamon candies
whipped cream for garnish (optional)
additional red cinnamon candies for garnish
    (optional)

In a medium saucepan, combine cider and cinnamon candies. Cook over medium heat, stirring occasionally, until mixture is hot and candy has melted. Pour into warm mugs. If desired, top each serving with a dollop of whipped cream sprinkled with cinnamon candies.

Hot Apple Pie

The creamy variation is less sweet than the full-whammy original. *See also* Tips for Making Hot Drinks, page 184.

SERVES 1

about 1 cup (8 oz.) apple juice

1 Tbsp. Ooey-Gooey Caramel Sauce, page 257, or store-bought caramel sauce

⅛ tsp. ground cinnamon

freshly grated nutmeg for garnish

In a small saucepan over medium heat, combine apple juice, caramel sauce, and cinnamon. Cook until mixture simmers, stirring to dissolve caramel sauce. Pour into a warm mug; garnish with a sprinkle of nutmeg.

VARIATION

Creamy Hot Apple Pie   Add 1 to 2 Tbsp. (½ to 1 oz.) whipping cream before heating. Top with a dollop of whipped cream sprinkled with nutmeg.

Ten

Nogs

NOG, WHICH is short for "eggnog," loosely describes any beverage made with beaten egg and usually milk or cream. The calorie count of almost any nog can be cut by substituting nonfat evaporated milk for the cream or whole milk, and by using 2 egg whites for each whole egg. The sweetness can be reduced and the texture lightened by folding in stiffly beaten egg whites just before serving. Never let eggnog sit at room temperature for more than 2 hours unless it's kept cold. The easy way to do that is to put the eggnog in a pitcher, then set the pitcher in a large bowl filled with ice. Leftover homemade eggnog should be tightly covered and refrigerated for use within 2 days. For information on eggs and egg safety, *see* the Ingredients Glossary section on eggs, page 23.

 Love and eggs are best when fresh.
—Russian proverb

Spiced Cream Nog

Add a tropical touch by substituting mango or papaya nectar for the orange juice.

SERVES 16

4 eggs or 1 cup egg substitute
2 medium ripe bananas, peeled and quartered
½ cup (4 oz.) fresh lemon juice
⅓ cup packed brown sugar
½ tsp. ground allspice
½ tsp. ground cinnamon
¼ tsp. freshly grated nutmeg
4 cups (32 oz.) fresh orange juice
1 quart vanilla ice cream, slightly softened
4 cups (32 oz.) chilled cream soda
1 orange, cut into ¼-inch slices

Combine eggs or egg substitute, bananas, lemon juice, sugar, spices, and 2 cups of the orange juice in a blender.

Cover and process at medium speed until smooth. Pour into a 2-quart container. Add remaining 2 cups orange juice; stir to combine. Cover and refrigerate for at least 4 hours or overnight. Just before serving, scoop softened ice cream into a punch bowl; stir until creamy. Add orange juice mixture, a third at a time, whisking after each addition. Slowly add cream soda, stirring gently to combine. Float orange slices on top. Serve in small glasses or punch cups.

Chocolate Eggnog

Warning: For dedicated chocoholics only!

SERVES 6 TO 8

2 cups (16 oz.) milk
4 eggs or 1 cup egg substitute
1 cup packed brown sugar
½ cup unsweetened cocoa powder
1 Tbsp. (½ oz.) pure vanilla extract
⅛ tsp. salt
1½ cups (12 oz.) whipping cream
about ⅓ cup grated semisweet chocolate for
    garnish

Combine milk, eggs or egg substitute, sugar, cocoa powder, vanilla, and salt in a blender. Cover and process at medium speed until smooth. Cover and refrigerate until just before serving, at least 2 hours so mixture becomes very cold. Whip cream to soft-peak stage. Pour chocolate mixture into a large bowl; gradually fold in whipped cream. Serve immediately in small glasses or punch cups; garnish with grated chocolate.

VARIATION

Mocha Eggnog Add 1 Tbsp. instant espresso powder to milk mixture before blending.

Quick Chocolate Eggnog

A chocolate lover's fix for prepared eggnog.

SERVES 1

1 cup chilled eggnog, store-bought or homemade
2 to 3 Tbsp. (1 to 1½ oz.) Dark Chocolate Syrup,
    page 256, or store-bought chocolate syrup
Chocolate Whipped Cream, (page 258), for
    garnish (optional)
freshly grated nutmeg

In a medium glass, briskly stir eggnog and chocolate syrup together. Top with whipped cream, if desired; sprinkle with nutmeg.

VARIATION

Quick Mocha Eggnog Add 1 tsp. instant espresso powder dissolved in 1 tsp. hot water.

✳ **Eggs are very much like small boys. If you overheat them or overbeat them, they will turn on you, and no amount of future love will right the wrong.**

—Irena Chalmers, Anglo-American author, wit, scholar

Eggnog for One

An individual eggnog for those times when nothing else will do. Since eggnog isn't traditionally served over ice, prechilled ingredients will produce a colder drink. Alternatively, the ingredients may be shaken with ice and strained into the glass, but that slightly dilutes the drink.

SERVES 1

1 egg or ¼ cup egg substitute

2 tsp. sugar

¼ tsp. pure vanilla extract

pinch of salt

1 cup (8 oz.) very cold milk

freshly grated nutmeg for garnish

Combine all ingredients except garnish in a blender. Cover and process at medium-low speed until smooth. Pour into a medium wineglass; sprinkle lightly with nutmeg.

VARIATION

Hot Nog   Beat egg or egg substitute, sugar, vanilla, and salt until frothy. Heat milk just until it simmers (do not boil). Gradually whisk milk into beaten egg mixture. Pour into a warm mug. *See also* Tips for Making Hot Drinks, page 184.

Egghead

SERVES 1

¾ cup (6 oz.) fresh orange juice
1 egg or ¼ cup egg substitute
¼ cup (2 oz.) milk or cream (optional)
3 ice cubes, coarsely crushed

Combine all ingredients in a blender. Cover and process at medium speed until smooth. Pour into a tall glass; add ice cubes.

✳ **A man who is stingy with the saffron is capable of seducing his own grandmother.**
—Norman Douglas, British writer

Vanilla-Saffron Silk

Saffron adds a seductive yet elusive flavor to this silky drink, which may be served cold or hot.

SERVES 4 TO 6

3 cups (24 oz.) milk
¾ cup sugar
4 threads saffron
pinch of salt
5 eggs or 1¼ cups egg substitute
1 Tbsp. (½ oz.) pure vanilla extract

In a medium saucepan over medium-low heat, combine milk, sugar, saffron, and salt. Cook, stirring occasionally, until mixture comes to a simmer. Remove from heat; cool to lukewarm, then refrigerate until very cold, 2 to 3 hours. Use a fork or spoon to retrieve saffron threads. Pour milk mixture into a blender. Add eggs or egg substitute and vanilla; cover and process at medium speed until smooth. Cover and refrigerate until ready to serve. Pour into medium wineglasses, sans ice.

VARIATION

Warm Vanilla-Saffron Silk   After milk mixture comes to a simmer, remove from heat and allow saffron to steep 15 minutes. Retrieve saffron threads with a fork or spoon. Return mixture to low heat and bring to a simmer. In a medium bowl, beat eggs or egg substitute until frothy. Whisk eggs into hot milk mixture; heat just until warm, stirring constantly. Mixture will become too thick if cooked too long (unless you're using egg substitute, which doesn't thicken when heated). If mixture separates (caused by the heat being too high), simply pour into a blender, cover, and process until smooth. To avoid spattering the hot liquid, start at low speed and gradually increase to high speed. Remove from heat; stir in vanilla. Pour into warm mugs and serve immediately. *See also* Tips for Making Hot Drinks, page 184.

Bananas Foster Nog

This potion is named after the classic New Orleans dish of bananas sautéed in a mixture of rum and brown sugar.

SERVES 8 TO 10

6 eggs or 1½ cups egg substitute

4 large ripe bananas, peeled and quartered

½ cup packed dark brown sugar

½ tsp. ground cinnamon

½ tsp. freshly grated nutmeg

4 cups (32 oz.) milk

¼ to ½ tsp. rum extract (optional)

1 quart caramel or praline ice cream, slightly
    softened

freshly grated nutmeg

Combine eggs or egg substitute, bananas, sugar, cinnamon, nutmeg, 2 cups of the milk, and rum extract, if desired, in a blender. Cover and process at medium speed until smooth. Pour into a 2-quart container; stir in remaining 2 cups milk. Cover and refrigerate for at least 4 hours or overnight. Just before serving, turn ice cream into a punch bowl; stir until creamy. Add banana mixture, a third at a time, whisking after each addition. Garnish with a sprinkle of nutmeg. Serve in small glasses or punch cups.

Mangoberry Nog

SERVES 2

1 cup (8 oz.) mango nectar
½ cup (4 oz.) milk
2 eggs or ½ cup egg substitute
1 pint fresh strawberries, washed and hulled
(reserve 2 unhulled berries for garnish)

Combine all ingredients in a blender. Cover and process at medium speed until smooth. Pour into tall glasses; garnish with reserved whole strawberries.

Old-Fashioned Party Eggnog

The brown sugar gives this nog a rich, caramel-like flavor. Granulated sugar may be substituted if preferred. Egg substitute can be substituted for the egg yolks, but not for the whites because the whites must be beaten until stiff—not possible with egg substitute.

SERVES 25

12 eggs, separated, or 1 cup egg substitute and 12 egg whites
1 cup packed dark brown sugar
8 cups (64 oz.) milk
1 Tbsp. (½ oz.) pure vanilla extract
4 cups (32 oz.) whipping cream
½ tsp. salt
freshly grated nutmeg

Beat egg yolks or egg substitute with the sugar until creamy and light. Stir in milk and vanilla; cover and refrigerate for at least 4 hours, or until very cold. Whip cream until it forms soft mounds; fold into eggnog mixture. May be refrigerated for 1 to 2 hours at this point. Just before serving, beat egg whites and salt to the soft-peak stage; fold into eggnog. Sprinkle with nutmeg. Serve in small glasses or punch cups.

Raspberry Noggin

This different take on eggnog is colorful and festive.

SERVES 16

6 eggs or 1½ cups egg substitute
2 cups (16 oz.) raspberry-flavored syrup
1 tsp. pure vanilla extract
½ tsp. freshly grated nutmeg
¼ tsp. salt
4 cups (32 oz.) milk
4 cups (32 oz.) whipping cream
1 quart raspberry ripple ice cream or raspberry
    sherbet, slightly softened
additional nutmeg for garnish

Combine eggs or egg substitute, syrup, vanilla, nutmeg, and salt in a blender. Cover and process at medium speed until smooth. Pour into a gallon container; stir in milk and cream. Cover and refrigerate for 2 hours, or until very cold. When ready to serve, turn ice cream into a punch bowl; stir until smooth. Gradually add raspberry eggnog mixture, whisking gently to combine. Sprinkle with nutmeg. Serve in small glasses or punch cups.

VARIATIONS

Raspberry-Orange Noggin   Substitute orange sherbet for the raspberry ice cream.

Orangeberry Noggin   Substitute Zesty Orange Syrup, page 253, or store-bought orange-flavored syrup for the raspberry-flavored syrup.

 Once in a young lifetime one should be allowed to have as much sweetness as one can possibly want and hold.

—Judith Olney, American food writer

Eggnog Smoothie Special

Chill all the ingredients so you won't have to dilute this drink with ice.

SERVES 1

1 cup (8 oz.) cold homemade eggnog or store-bought eggnog

1 cup chilled chopped fruit (bananas, strawberries, peaches, and so on)

½ tsp. pure vanilla extract

Combine all ingredients in a blender. Cover and process at high speed until smooth. Pour into a tall glass; garnish with a slice of the fruit used in the drink.

Honey-Lemon Nog

Refreshing and soothing and not too sweet. The warm version is like a hug in a mug.

SERVES 1

1 cup (8 oz.) milk

1 egg or ¼ cup egg substitute

2 Tbsp. (1 oz.) Honey-Lemon Syrup, page 254, or 1
     Tbsp. (½ oz.) *each* honey and fresh lemon juice

⅛ tsp. ground cinnamon

Combine all ingredients in a blender. Cover and process
at high speed until smooth. Pour into a tall glass; add ice
cubes, if desired.

VARIATION

Warm Honey-Lemon Nog   In a small saucepan, beat
egg, syrup, cinnamon, and about ¼ cup (2 oz.) of the milk
until smooth. Stir in remaining milk. Cook over low heat,
stirring constantly, until mixture is hot. Pour into warm
mug. *See also* Tips for Making Hot Drinks, page 184.

Low-Fat Eggnog

Cooking this mixture thickens it slightly, making the texture more velvety, like those naughty nogs made with
cream. Egg substitute cannot be used in this nog because it
won't thicken the mixture properly.

SERVES 8

6 eggs

½ cup sugar

¾ tsp. freshly grated nutmeg

4 cups (32 oz.) nonfat milk

1 12-oz. can evaporated nonfat milk

2 tsp. pure vanilla extract

freshly grated nutmeg for garnish

In a heavy, medium saucepan, whisk eggs, sugar, and nutmeg until frothy; gradually stir in both types of milk. Cook over low heat, stirring constantly, until mixture thickens slightly. Immediately remove from heat. Set pan in a bowl of ice water; stir until mixture cools. Stir in vanilla. Cover and refrigerate until chilled, at least 4 hours. Just before serving, whisk until frothy. Serve in punch cups; dust each serving lightly with nutmeg.

VARIATION

Low-Fat Chocolate Eggnog   Increase sugar to ⅔ cup and mix well with ¼ cup unsweetened cocoa powder before adding eggs and nutmeg.

Eleven

Punches

P UNCHES CAN be hot or cold and are typically made in large quantities (though there are exceptions to this rule).

Although most punches are served in a punch bowl, many can be made and served from a pitcher. For cold punches, start with chilled ingredients if you're in a hurry. For hot punches, always preheat the punch bowl by filling it with hot water and letting stand for a few minutes; dry thoroughly before using. Punch cups typically hold 6 ounces.

A large watermelon makes a great "organic" punch bowl for cold punches. Cut 1½-inch zigzags horizontally all around the melon and about a third down from the top.

Lift off the top third. If the bottom part of the watermelon doesn't sit securely upright, slice a tiny portion off the bottom so it will sit flat. Use a large spoon to scoop out the flesh of your watermelon punch bowl, being careful to leave sturdy 1-inch sides and bottom. Refrigerate the watermelon punch bowl until ready to use.

Hot Punches

Glögg [GLUHG; GLOEG]

This is the nonalcoholic version of a traditional Swedish spiced wine punch that's particularly popular during Advent. Making glögg a day ahead of time allows the flavors to mellow and intensify. *See also* Tips for Making Hot Drinks, page 184.

SERVES 12

zest from 2 medium oranges
20 cardamom seeds
15 whole cloves
2 cinnamon sticks, broken into 1-inch pieces
1 cup sugar
1½ cups raisins
1½ cups whole blanched almonds
3 (750 ml) bottles of dealcoholized red wine

Place orange zest, cardamom seeds, cloves, and cinnamon sticks in the center of a square of double-thick cheesecloth; use a string to tie them securely into a bag. (Or put the spices and zest in a large, covered tea infuser.) Put spice bag or infuser in a large pot (not aluminum) with sugar, raisins, almonds, and wine; bring to a boil over medium heat, stirring occasionally. Reduce heat to low; simmer, uncovered, for 20 minutes. Remove from heat; cool to room temperature. Cover and refrigerate overnight for flavors to mellow. Just before serving, remove spice bag. Heat glögg until very hot. Pour into a large, heatproof punch bowl. Ladle into heatproof punch cups or small mugs, adding a few raisins and almonds to each serving. Leftover glögg can be tightly covered and refrigerated for at least 1 month.

Mulled Cider

Make several batches of this spicy drink to have on hand when company drops in. For a pretty garnish, stud tiny apples with cloves and float them in the punch bowl. *See also* Tips for Making Hot Drinks, page 184.

SERVES 8

8 cups (64 oz.) apple cider
juice and zest from 1 large orange
juice and zest from 1 large lemon
¼ cup (2 oz.) honey
12 whole cloves
4 cinnamon sticks
½ tsp. freshly grated nutmeg

Combine all ingredients in a large pot (not aluminum); bring to a simmer over medium heat, stirring occasionally. Reduce heat to low; simmer for 10 minutes. Pour into a

large, heatproof punch bowl. Ladle into heatproof punch
cups or small mugs. Leftover mulled cider can be tightly
covered and refrigerated for at least 1 month.

VARIATION

Mulled Cranberry Cup   Substitute cranberry juice for
the apple çider.

Hot Tea Party Punch

You can make this punch a day or two ahead of time and
reheat at the last minute. *See also* Tips for Making Hot
Drinks, page 184.

SERVES 8

6 cups (48 oz.) water
8 black currant or orange-spice tea bags
⅓ cup sugar
2 cinnamon sticks
10 whole cloves
1 6-oz. can frozen cranberry-apple juice
     concentrate
1½ cups (12 oz.) fresh orange juice
6 to 8 orange slices for garnish

In a large saucepan, combine water, tea bags, sugar,
cinnamon, and cloves. Bring to a boil, stirring to dissolve
sugar. Remove from heat; cover and let steep 15

minutes. Remove tea bags, squeezing to extract as much liquid as possible. Stir in frozen juice concentrate and fresh orange juice. If serving immediately, reheat until simmering. Pour into a heatproof punch bowl; float orange slices on top. Ladle into heatproof punch cups. If making ahead, cover and refrigerate; heat just before serving.

Cider House Grog

Traditional grog is a rum-based drink named after eighteenth-century British Admiral Edward Vernon who, because he wore a thick grogram cape, was nicknamed "Old Grog." This version, sweetened with maple syrup, is sure to warm the cockles of the coldest heart. *See also* Tips for Making Hot Drinks, page 184.

SERVES 12

8 cups (64 oz.) apple cider
¾ cup (6 oz.) pure maple syrup
2 cups (16 oz.) fresh orange juice
½ cup (4 oz.) fresh lemon juice
1 Tbsp. whole cloves
1 tsp. rum extract (optional)
1 large apple, cored and cut into ¼-inch-thick
    slices, for garnish

In a large pot, combine all ingredients except apple slices; bring to a boil. Simmer, uncovered, for 20 minutes, stirring occasionally. Pour into a heatproof punch bowl; drop in apple slices. Serve in heatproof punch cups or small mugs.

Warm Milk Punch

This drink tastes like a warm eggnog without the eggs. Cover and refrigerate leftover punch for up to 5 days; reheat it whenever you need a hug. *See also* Tips for Making Hot Drinks, page 184.

SERVES 8

2 cinnamon sticks, broken in half
12 whole cloves
1 tsp. fennel seeds
1 tsp. whole allspice berries
4 cups (32 oz.) milk
4 cups (32 oz.) half & half
½ cup packed brown sugar
1 Tbsp. (½ oz.) pure vanilla extract
1 tsp. pure almond extract
2 tsp. rum extract (optional)
freshly grated nutmeg for garnish

Place cinnamon, cloves, fennel, and allspice in the center of a square of double-thick cheesecloth; use a string to tie securely into a bag. (Or put spices in a large, covered tea infuser.) Put spice bag or infuser in a large saucepan;

add milk, half & half, and sugar. Bring mixture to a simmer. Cook over low heat, uncovered, for 10 minutes, stirring often. Remove spice bag. Stir in vanilla, almond, and rum extracts. Serve in mugs; garnish with a dusting of nutmeg.

Cranberry Wassail Bowl [WAH-suhl]

The classic wassail is an ale-based punch spiked with sherry and brandy. This rendition contains no alcoholic ingredients, of course, but stays in the spirit with the spices and baked apples—the cranberry juice gives it festive flair. The word "wassail" also refers to a toast, hailing back to the old English custom of saluting the health of those at a celebration by passing a bowl of spiced ale from which each person would drink and then say *Wass hael*, Saxon for "Be whole" or "Be healthy." A *wassailer* is one who does the toasting or drinking. *See also* Tips for Making Hot Drinks, page 184.

SERVES 12

12 tiny tart apples
6 cups (48 oz.) cranberry juice
4 cups (32 oz.) apple juice
½ cup packed brown sugar
juice and peel of 2 large oranges
juice and peel of 2 large lemons

1 tsp. *each* ground nutmeg, allspice, and cinnamon

½ tsp. *each* ground ginger and cloves

Place apples on an ungreased baking sheet; bake in a preheated 350°F oven for 30 minutes. Remove from oven and set aside. In a large pot (not aluminum), combine remaining ingredients; bring to a boil over medium heat, stirring occasionally. Reduce heat to low; simmer for 20 minutes. Strain into a large, heatproof punch bowl, discarding citrus peel; add baked apples. Serve in heatproof punch cups or small mugs, adding an apple to each serving. Leftover wassail (apples removed) can be tightly covered and refrigerated for at least 1 month.

Cold Punches

Ginger Beer Punch

This nonalcoholic ginger beer is exceedingly refreshing and makes a great accompaniment for spicy dishes.

SERVES 16

2 4-inch pieces (½ inch in diameter) peeled ginger, cut into 8 pieces

12 cups (96 oz.) water

2 cups sugar

zest and juice of 3 large lemons

ice mold or block (*see* Punch-Bowl Ice, page 260) (optional)

4 cups (32 oz.) chilled ginger ale

16 fresh peeled or candied ginger slices for garnish (optional)

Place ginger on a cutting board and use a mallet or other heavy utensil to pulverize it. Put ginger (along with any exuded juices) into a large pot. Add water, sugar, and lemon zest and juice; stir to combine. Bring to a boil over medium heat. Reduce heat to low; cover and simmer for 30 minutes. Cool to room temperature. Strain and refrigerate for up to 2 weeks.

To serve in a punch bowl: At least a day ahead of time, make an ice ring (page 260) with fruit and ginger slices in it. Just before serving, pour ginger beer mixture into punch bowl. Slowly stir in ginger ale; add ice ring. Serve in tall, ice-filled glasses; garnish with ginger slices, if desired.

To serve individually: Put 3 to 4 ice cubes in a tall glass; fill glass three-quarters full with chilled ginger beer; top with ginger ale, stirring gently. Garnish with a ginger slice, if desired.

Syllabub [SIHL-uh-bub]

The name of this creamy, wine-flavored concoction is said to have originated during Elizabethan times; it's a combination of the words *sille* (a French wine once used in the libation) and *bub*, old English slang for "bubbling drink."

SERVES 8

3 cups (24 oz.) milk
2 cups (16 oz.) whipping cream
1¼ cups superfine sugar, divided
finely grated zest and juice from 1½ medium
     lemons
¼ tsp. salt
2 cups (16 oz.) chilled dealcoholized white wine

4 egg whites, room temperature
freshly grated nutmeg

Combine milk, cream, 1 cup of the sugar, lemon zest and juice, and salt in a blender. Cover and process at medium speed until frothy. Pour into a punch bowl; stir in wine. Beat egg whites until soft peaks form. Gradually add remaining ¼ cup sugar, beating until whites are glossy and stiff. Use a tablespoon to drop mounds of the meringue onto the surface of the syllabub. Dust each mound lightly with nutmeg. Serve in punch cups, topping each serving with a meringue puff.

Posset [POSS-iht]

A hearty custard-based drink that was immensely popular in the Middle Ages, in part because it was considered a restorative. Apple juice can be substituted for the dealcoholized wine, if desired.

SERVES 8

8 eggs
⅔ cup sugar
¾ tsp. freshly grated nutmeg
4 cups (32 oz.) milk
1½ cups (12 oz.) dealcoholized white wine
freshly grated nutmeg for garnish

In a heavy, medium saucepan, beat eggs, sugar, and nutmeg until frothy; gradually stir in milk. Cook over low heat, stirring constantly, until mixture thickly coats a metal spoon. Remove from heat. Set pan in a bowl of ice water; stir custard until it's lukewarm. Stir in wine. Cover and refrigerate until chilled, at least 2 hours. Serve in punch cups; dust each serving lightly with nutmeg.

West Indies Pineapple Pleaser

If falernum is unavailable, you can substitute Ginger-Lime Syrup, page 254.

SERVES 10

4 cups (32 oz.) pineapple juice
⅔ cup (scant 6 oz.) fresh lime juice
⅔ cup (scant 6 oz.) falernum
5 cups (40 oz.) chilled lime-flavored sparkling
water
10 lime slices for garnish

In a large pitcher, mix pineapple juice, lime juice, and falernum, stirring to combine. Cover and refrigerate until ready to use. Just before serving, gently stir in sparkling water. Pour into tall, ice-filled glasses; garnish with lime slices.

Cider Cup

Although this libation is liquor-free, classic "cups" are chilled punches made with wine or champagne plus brandy and an orange-flavored liqueur. Cups are traditionally garnished with fruit slices and often cucumber peel.

SERVES 8

4 cups (32 oz.) chilled apple cider or apple juice
¾ cup (6 oz.) chilled strong tea
½ cup (4 oz.) fresh orange juice or nonalcoholic
    Triple Sec or orange-flavored syrup
1½ cups (12 oz.) chilled seltzer water or club soda
1½ Tbsp. powdered sugar
8 apple slices, brushed lightly with lemon juice, for
    garnish
8 mint sprigs for garnish

Fill a large glass pitcher halfway with ice cubes. Add all ingredients except garnishes; stir gently. Pour into punch cups or wineglasses; garnish each serving with apple slice and mint.

Sangría [san-GREE-uh]

The word *sangría* comes from the Spanish *sangre* ("blood"), after the color of the classic red-wine sangría. *Sangría blanca* ("white") is the white-wine version.

SERVES 10

2 (750 ml) bottles chilled dealcoholized
   red wine
2 cups (16 oz.) chilled fresh orange juice
³/₈ cup (3 oz.) fresh lemon or lime juice
2 cups (16 oz.) chilled seltzer water,
   club soda, or citrus-flavored mineral
   water
about ½ cup superfine sugar
ice mold or block (see Punch-Bowl Ice, page 260)
   (optional)
1 orange, sliced
1 lemon, sliced

Pour wine, orange juice, and lemon or lime juice into a
punch bowl. Stir in seltzer; sweeten to taste with sugar.
Add ice mold, if desired, and fruit slices. Serve in
medium-size stemmed, ice-filled glasses.

VARIATIONS

Sangría Blanca   Substitute dealcoholized white
wine for the red wine, and peach slices for the sliced
orange.

Sparkling Sangría   Substitute dealcoholized
sparkling white or red wine for the red wine.
Along with the orange and lemon slices, add about 15
green grapes.

✳ **Tomatoes are lusty enough, yet there runs through tomatoes an undercurrent of frivolity.**
—Tom Robbins, American novelist

Sangrita [san-GREE-tuh]

Although sometimes confused with sangría (page 226), sangrita's tomato–orange juice base and hot-pepper kick clearly set it apart. Traditionally, sangrita is served as a chaser to a tequila shot, but here I offer it as an alcohol-free punch, perfect for brunches and lunches. This concoction is supposed to be snappy, so don't stint on the Tabasco sauce.

SERVES 8 TO 10

6 cups (48 oz.) tomato juice
3 cups (24 oz.) fresh orange juice
1 cup (8 oz.) fresh lime juice
2 Tbsp. (1 oz.) Worcestershire sauce
1 to 2 Tbsp. (½ to 1 oz.) green Tabasco sauce
1½ tsp. celery salt
salt
8 to 10 orange slices for garnish

Combine the first 6 ingredients in a large pitcher, stirring to mix well. Salt to taste. Cover and refrigerate for at least 2 hours. Serve in tall, ice-filled glasses; garnish with orange slices.

VARIATION

Hot Sangrita Combine ingredients in a large saucepan; bring to a simmer over medium heat. Pour into warm mugs; garnish with orange slices. *See also* Tips for Making Hot Drinks, page 184.

Orange Whammy

SERVES 8

2 cups (16 oz.) fresh orange juice
1 15-oz. can mandarin oranges, drained
¼ tsp. orange-flower water (optional)
2 pints orange sherbet, slightly softened, divided
4 cups (32 oz.) chilled plain or orange-flavored
    sparkling water

Combine orange juice, oranges, and orange-flower water, if desired, in a blender. Cover and process at high speed until oranges are puréed. Add 1 pint sherbet; blend at medium speed until smooth. Pour into a punch bowl; slowly stir in sparkling water. Add small scoops of remaining 1 pint sherbet (the scoops will float). Serve immediately in punch cups or small wineglasses.

Tahitian Sunset

SERVES 14

2 pints strawberries, washed

2 11.5-oz. cans mango nectar

2 11.5-oz. cans guava nectar

1 11.5-oz. can papaya nectar

2 14-oz. cans low-fat coconut milk

4 cups (32 oz.) chilled ginger ale

Reserve 14 whole strawberries; hull remaining berries. Working in batches, combine some of the strawberries with nectars and coconut milk in a blender. Cover and process at high speed until smooth. Pour each batch into a very large pitcher. Stir final mixture well. For each serving, place 4 ice cubes into a tall glass; fill three-quarters full with punch mixture. Top with ginger ale, stirring gently; garnish each glass with one of the reserved whole strawberries.

Minted Melonita

Cantaloupe and Crenshaw melons can also be used in this refresher.

SERVES 8

1 (3 pound) honeydew melon, seeded and cut into
    chunks (4 to 5 cups)

¼ cup fresh mint leaves (packed)
4 cups (32 oz.) fresh orange juice
superfine sugar
mint sprigs for garnish

Remove melon flesh from rind; cut into 1-inch pieces. In a blender, combine mint, 1 cup of the orange juice, and enough melon to fill jar halfway. Cover and process at medium-high speed until smooth. Pour into a large pitcher. Blend remaining melon and orange juice in batches until smooth, adding each batch to pitcher. Add sugar to taste. Cover and refrigerate until ready to serve. Stir well before serving. Pour into tall, ice-filled glasses; garnish with mint sprigs.

✳ **Success to me is having ten honeydew melons and eating only the top half of each one.**
—Barbra Streisand, American singer, actress, filmmaker

Kiss-Me-Quick Punch

This pale, sparkling punch is lightly sweet, but can be made sweeter with the addition of more orgeat syrup, sugar syrup, or superfine sugar.

SERVES 12

4 cups (32 oz.) white grape–kiwi juice
3 cups (24 oz.) strongly brewed green tea

½ cup (4 oz.) fresh lemon juice

½ cup (4 oz.) orgeat syrup

1 (750 ml) bottle chilled dealcoholized sparkling
  white wine

ice mold or block (*see* Punch-Bowl Ice, page 260)
  (optional)

1 to 2 washed, unpeeled kiwifruit, cut into ¼-inch
  slices, for garnish

Combine the first 4 ingredients; cover and refrigerate
until very cold, at least 2 hours. Just before serving,
pour mixture into a punch bowl. Slowly add sparkling
wine, stirring gently. Add ice mold and kiwi slices. Serve
in punch cups or small wineglasses.

Red Satin Punch

For a festive touch, embellish an ice mold (*see* Decorated
Ice Mold, page 261) with raspberries or cranberries.

SERVES 20

1 12-oz. can frozen cranberry-raspberry juice
  concentrate, thawed

4 cups (32 oz.) water

½ cup (4 oz.) grenadine

1 quart raspberry or strawberry sherbet, slightly
  softened

2 (750 ml) bottles chilled dealcoholized sparkling
   red wine
ice mold or block (*see* Punch-Bowl Ice, page 260)
   (optional)

In a large pitcher, stir together juice concentrate, water, and grenadine. Refrigerate until very cold, about 2 hours. Just before serving, turn sherbet into a punch bowl; stir to soften. Add juice mixture, stirring well to combine. Slowly add sparkling wine, stirring gently; add ice mold. Serve in punch cups or wineglasses.

Twelve

Mocktails

Cocktails with a Twist

COCKTAILS AND cocktailing are back in a big way, but that doesn't mean alcohol has to be involved. This chapter includes everything from variations on originals like Kir, Fuzzy Navel, and Cosmopolitan to old-fashioned favorites such as Shirley Temple and Roy Rogers. The section on Tips for Making Great Drinks, page 10, gives techniques for creating mocktails that look and taste professional. While you don't need a bevy of various-size glasses to make your drinks look terrific, having a few wouldn't hurt. Here are some that would fit the bill for most drinks: cocktail glasses (also called *martini glasses*), champagne flutes or medium wineglasses, short (6 ounces) old-fashioned glasses, and tall (12 to 14 ounces) glasses. See Glassware, page 5, for more details.

 Being sober for so many years is getting interesting.
—Peter O'Toole, British actor

Apricot Cobbler

Cobblers date back to at least 1809, and were originally made with sherry—this version uses dealcoholized white wine. Any fruit juice can be substituted for the apricot nectar—cranberry juice turns this drink into a Cranberry Cobbler.

SERVES 1

⅓ cup (scant 3 oz.) apricot nectar
⅓ cup (scant 3 oz.) dealcoholized sparkling white
    wine or seltzer water
maraschino cherry for garnish

Fill a wineglass three-quarters full with cracked or crushed ice. Add apricot nectar and wine or seltzer; stir gently. Garnish with cherry.

Is There an "Ape" in Apricot?

D o y o u say APE-rih-kaht or AP-rih-kaht? Well, according to Charles Harrington Elster's *There Is No Zoo in Zoology,* the second (short A) version has been preferred since about 1970, when dictionaries gradually began to shift to this more common pronunciation. But don't worry if you're a longtime "ape"-ricot articulator—this variant pronunciation is perfectly acceptable.

Blameless Bloody Bull

Using spicy tomato juice or V-8 juice adds pizzazz to this drink.

SERVES 1

½ cup (4 oz.) tomato or V-8 juice
⅜ cup (3 oz.) beef broth, beef bouillon, or beef consommé
1½ tsp. fresh lemon juice
⅛ tsp. black pepper
3 ice cubes
lime wedge for garnish

Shake all ingredients except garnish with ice. Pour into an old-fashioned glass. Add ice cubes; garnish with lime wedge.

Cosmopolitan (Cosmo)

For an added touch of sweetness and a professional look, moisten the rim of a glass with lime juice, then dip in granulated sugar.

SERVES 1

3 Tbsp. (1½ oz.) nonalcoholic Triple Sec or orange-
     flavored syrup
3 Tbsp. (1½ oz.) cranberry juice
1 Tbsp. (½ oz.) fresh lime juice
lime slice for garnish

Shake all ingredients except garnish with ice; strain into a martini glass. Garnish with lime slice.

Fuzzless Navel

The nonalcoholic version of the Fuzzy Navel, which uses peach Schnapps.

SERVES 1

¾ cup (6 oz.) fresh orange juice
⅓ cup (scant 3 oz.) peach nectar
orange slice for garnish

Combine orange juice and peach nectar in a
tall glass; stir. Add ice cubes; garnish with orange slice.

Guava Lava

SERVES 1

½ cup (4 oz.) guava nectar
1 Tbsp. (½ oz.) heavy cream
2 tsp. fresh lime juice
3 ice cubes, coarsely crushed

Combine all ingredients in a blender. Cover and
process at high speed until smooth. Pour into a
champagne flute.

Kir

This apéritif is said to have been named after Canon Félix
Kir, a famous French war hero who was also mayor of
Dijon. The more black currant syrup you use, the sweeter
the drink.

SERVES 1

½ to 2 tsp. black currant (cassis) syrup
about ¾ cup (6 oz.) chilled dealcoholized white
wine
lemon twist for garnish

Pour black currant syrup into a chilled
champagne flute. Slowly add wine; drop in lemon
twist.

VARIATIONS

Kir Royale   Substitute sparkling white wine for the still wine.

Holiday Kir   Substitute grenadine for the black currant syrup.

 I envy people who drink—at least they know what to blame everything on.

—Oscar Levant, American composer, pianist

Maiden Madras

Serve this alcohol-free version of a Madras cocktail and no one will even miss the vodka.

SERVES 1

½ cup (4 oz.) cranberry juice
⅜ cup (3 oz.) fresh orange juice
orange slice for garnish

Pour juices into a tall glass filled with ice cubes; stir well. Garnish with orange slice.

Margarita

The margarita dates back to the early 1930s and, by most accounts, it hails from Mexico. Frosting the rim of the glass (*see* page 10) is traditional but certainly not necessary. You can easily find inexpensive margarita glasses, but this drink will taste just as good served in a wineglass.

SERVES 1

½ cup (4 oz.) dealcoholized white wine
¼ cup (2 oz.) fresh lime juice
2 Tbsp. (1 oz.) nonalcoholic Triple Sec or orange-flavored syrup
lime wedge or slice for garnish

Moisten a margarita glass or wineglass rim with a little lime juice, then dip rim into salt. Shake the first 3 ingredients with cracked ice; strain into glass. Garnish with lime wedge.

VARIATIONS

Frozen Margarita Combine all ingredients except garnish in a blender. Add 1 cup crushed ice. Cover and process at medium speed until slushy. Garnish with lime.

Frozen Fruit Margarita Combine all ingredients except garnish in a blender. Add ½ cup crushed ice and ¾ cup frozen fruit slices or chunks (peach, mango, melon, strawberries, and so on). Cover and process at medium speed until slushy. Garnish with lime or a slice or chunk of the fruit you use.

Favorite Fruit Margarita   Substitute your favorite fruit-flavored syrup for the Triple Sec. Garnish with lime or a wedge of fruit of the same flavor as the syrup.

Orange Margarita   Substitute fresh orange juice for the wine. Garnish with orange slice.

Mimosa

This brunch favorite is refreshing and light.

SERVES 1

½ cup (4 oz.) chilled fresh orange juice
½ cup (4 oz.) chilled dealcoholized sparkling white wine
½ orange slice for garnish

Pour orange juice into a champagne flute. Slowly add sparkling wine; stir gently. Garnish with orange slice.

Mockquila Sunrise

A takeoff on the famous Tequila Sunrise. Because grenadine is heavier than the other ingredients in this drink, it sinks to the bottom, creating a red "sunrise" effect that contrasts dramatically with the golden orange juice.

SERVES 1

about ¾ cup (6 oz.) fresh orange
    juice

1 to 2 Tbsp. (½ to 1 oz.) grenadine
orange slice for garnish

Place 3 to 4 ice cubes in a tall glass; pour in orange juice
to within 1½ inches of glass rim. Add grenadine, letting
it settle to the bottom of the glass (do not stir). Garnish
with orange slice.

Naked Bullshot

The name has nothing to do with nudity, but rather with
the fact that this classic drink is sans its usual vodka or gin.

SERVES 1

½ cup (4 oz.) chilled beef bouillon or broth
¼ cup (2 oz.) water
1 tsp. fresh lemon juice
½ tsp. Worcestershire sauce
2 dashes (about ⅛ tsp.) Tabasco sauce
salt and freshly ground pepper
lemon slice for garnish

Pour bouillon, water, lemon juice, and Worcestershire and
Tabasco sauces into a tall glass. Add salt and pepper
to taste; stir well. Add ice cubes; garnish with lemon slice.

VARIATIONS

Cock 'n' Bull Shot   Substitute ¼ cup (2 oz.) chilled
chicken bouillon or broth for ¼ cup of the beef bouillon.

Hot Bullshot In a small saucepan, combine all ingredients except garnish; bring to a boil. Pour into a warm mug; add lemon slice. *See also* Tips for Making Hot Drinks, page 184.

Peaches and Cream

Any fruit nectar can be used for this drink—try apricot, strawberry, or mango for a change of pace.

> SERVES 1
>
> ½ cup (4 oz.) peach nectar
> 2 Tbsp. (1 oz.) heavy cream
>
> Shake ingredients with ice; strain into a cocktail glass.

 "I never drink—wine." (said by Count Dracula)
—Bram Stoker, British novelist

Planter's Punch

The original Planter's Punch was created by the Myers Rum Company in the late 1800s to market their rum. This nonalcoholic version is equally wonderful.

> SERVES 1
>
> 1 cup (8 oz.) fresh orange juice
> 1 Tbsp. (½ oz.) fresh lemon or lime juice

2 tsp. powdered sugar

2 tsp. grenadine

1 to 2 drops rum extract (optional)

orange slice for garnish

maraschino cherry for garnish

Shake all ingredients except garnishes with ice. Strain into a tall, ice-filled glass. Garnish with orange slice and cherry; serve with a straw.

Roy Rogers

SERVES 1

¼ cup (2 oz.) fresh orange juice

1 Tbsp. (½ oz.) grenadine

¾ cup (6 oz.) chilled ginger ale

maraschino cherry for garnish

Pour orange juice and grenadine into a tall, ice-filled glass. Top with ginger ale, stirring gently; garnish with cherry.

Safe Sex on the Beach

A nonalcoholic rendition of the wildly popular Sex on the Beach.

SERVES 1

⅜ cup (3 oz.) cranberry juice

⅜ cup (3 oz.) fresh orange juice or

unsweetened grapefruit
juice
2 Tbsp. (1 oz.) peach nectar
maraschino cherry for garnish

Pour all ingredients except garnish into a tall glass; stir well. Add ice; garnish with cherry.

Sea Breeze

SERVES 1

½ cup (4 oz.) unsweetened grapefruit juice
½ cup (4 oz.) cranberry juice
lime wedge for garnish

Pour juices into a tall glass two-thirds full of ice cubes; mix well. Garnish with lime wedge.

Shirley Temple

One of the original nonalcoholic cocktails, named for the famous child actor of the 1930s, who later in life (as Shirley Temple Black) gained a different kind of fame as a United States diplomat.

SERVES 1

¾ cup (6 oz.) chilled ginger ale
1 to 2 tsp. grenadine

orange slice for garnish
maraschino cherry for garnish

Gently stir together ginger ale and grenadine in a
wineglass. Add ice cubes; garnish with orange slice and
cherry.

✳ **It's all right to drink like a fish—
if you drink what a fish drinks.**

—Mary Pettibone Poole, American writer

Slinky

SERVES 1

½ cup (4 oz.) apricot nectar
¼ cup (2 oz.) fresh orange juice
1 Tbsp. (½ oz.) fresh lemon juice
lemon twist for garnish

Shake all ingredients except garnish with ice; strain into
a cocktail glass. Drop in lemon twist.

Sober Clam Digger

Clamato juice, a commercial blend of clam and tomato
juices, is available in supermarkets.

SERVES 1

1 cup (8 oz.) Clamato juice (or ½ cup (4 oz.) *each*
    tomato juice and clam juice)
2 tsp. fresh lemon juice
¼ tsp. Tabasco sauce
¼ tsp. Worcestershire sauce
pinch of freshly ground pepper
lemon slice for garnish

Shake all ingredients except garnish with ice. Strain into a tall, ice-filled glass; garnish with lemon slice.

Tiña Colada [TEEN-yah koh-LAH-dah]

This drink is adapted from Piña Colada, whose name is Spanish for "strained pineapple."

SERVES 1

¾ cup (6 oz.) unsweetened pineapple juice
¼ cup (2 oz.) cream of coconut
4 ice cubes, coarsely crushed
pineapple spear or toasted coconut, page 259, for
    garnish

Combine pineapple juice, cream of coconut, and ice in a blender. Cover and process at high speed until smooth. Pour into a tall glass; garnish with pineapple spear or toasted coconut or both.

Virgin Mary

The original Bloody Mary was created in 1921 by Pete Petiot, a bartender at Harry's New York Bar in Paris.

SERVES 1

¾ cup (6 oz.) tomato juice
1 Tbsp. (½ oz.) fresh lemon juice
¼ tsp. Worcestershire sauce
⅛ to ¼ tsp. Tabasco sauce
pinch of celery salt
pinch of black pepper
salt to taste
½ tsp. horseradish (optional)
celery stalk with leaves or lime wedge for garnish

Shake all ingredients except garnish with ice. Strain into a tall glass; garnish with celery or lime.

Thirteen

Lagniappe

[lan-YAP] Something Extra or
Unexpected

Sugar Syrup

Also called "simple syrup," this mixture
of sugar and water is particularly useful
for sweetening iced drinks, where granulated sugar might dissolve slowly. To
sweeten a drink, use 1½ times as much
sugar syrup as sugar.

MAKES ABOUT 2¾ CUPS

2 cups (16 oz.) water
2 cups sugar

In a medium saucepan, stir ingredients together. Bring to a boil, stirring occasionally. Immediately reduce heat to low. Simmer, uncovered and without stirring, for 10 minutes. Cool to room temperature. Transfer to a container with a tight lid. Cover and refrigerate indefinitely.

VARIATIONS

Spiced Syrup Add 10 whole cloves, 2 cinnamon sticks, and 20 whole allspice before beginning to heat. Strain just before refrigerating.

Coffee Syrup Substitute prepared double-strength coffee for the water, or dissolve 1 rounded Tbsp. instant espresso powder in 2 cups water.

Ginger Syrup

MAKES ABOUT 1⅓ CUPS

1½ cups (12 oz.) water
1½ cups sugar
1 6-inch piece (½ inch in diameter) peeled ginger, finely chopped

In a medium saucepan, stir ingredients together. Bring to a boil, stirring occasionally. Immediately reduce heat to low. Simmer, uncovered and without stirring, for 10 minutes. Cool to room temperature. Strain into a container with a tight lid. Cover and refrigerate for up to 2 weeks.

Zesty Lemon Syrup

The lemon zest adds pizzazz to this syrup, which is great for any number of refreshers, including Old-Fashioned Lemonade (*see* page 72), lemon ice cream sodas, and lemon spritzers (*see* page 70).

MAKES ABOUT 3½ CUPS

1½ cups (12 oz.) water
2 cups sugar
3 Tbsp. lemon zest
1½ cups (12 oz.) fresh lemon juice

In a medium saucepan, stir water, sugar, and lemon zest together. Bring to a boil, stirring occasionally. Immediately reduce heat to low. Simmer, uncovered and without stirring, for 10 minutes. Cool to room temperature. Strain into a container with a tight lid; stir in lemon juice. Cover and refrigerate for up to 1 month.

VARIATIONS

Zesty Orange Syrup   Reduce water to 1 cup (8 oz.), substitute grated zest from 2 large oranges for the lemon zest, and 2 cups (24 oz.) fresh orange juice for the 1½ cups lemon juice.

Zesty Lemon-Orange Syrup   Reduce lemon zest to 2 Tbsp., add 2 Tbsp. orange zest; reduce lemon juice to ½ cup (4 oz.), add 1 cup (8 oz.) fresh orange juice.

Zesty Lime Syrup   Substitute ¼ cup lime zest for the lemon zest, and fresh lime juice for the lemon juice.

Zesty Grapefruit Syrup   Substitute grated zest from 2 large grapefruits for the lemon zest, and fresh grapefruit juice for the lemon juice.

Ginger-Lime Syrup

This syrup is a good substitute for falernum (*see* page 25).

MAKES ABOUT 1⅓ CUPS

1 cup (8 oz.) fresh lime juice

1 cup sugar

¼ cup peeled ginger slices

½ tsp. pure almond extract

In a medium saucepan, stir lime juice, sugar, and ginger together. Bring to a boil, stirring occasionally. Immediately reduce heat to low. Simmer, uncovered and without stirring, for 10 minutes. Cool to room temperature. Remove ginger with a slotted spoon. Stir in almond extract. Transfer to a container with a tight lid. Cover and refrigerate for up to 1 month.

Honey-Lemon Syrup

The perfect sweetener for hot or iced tea.

MAKES 1 CUP

½ cup (4 oz.) honey

½ cup (4 oz.) fresh lemon juice

In a small saucepan over low heat, stir ingredients together until smooth and well combined. Cool to room temperature. Transfer to a container with a tight lid. Cover and refrigerate for up to 2 weeks.

VARIATION

Maple-Lemon Syrup   Substitute pure maple syrup for the honey.

Minted Citrus Syrup

A kiss of fresh mint (and don't even think of using dried leaves) gives this syrup the taste of summer. Use it for ice cream sodas (*see* Kiss O' Citrus Soda, page 129), or mix it with sparkling water and ice for a light, refreshing spritzer.

MAKES ABOUT 1¼ CUPS

1 cup sugar

1 cup (8 oz.) fresh orange, lemon, lime, or grapefruit juice

½ cup chopped fresh mint

1 Tbsp. minced ginger

In a medium saucepan, stir ingredients together. Bring to a boil, stirring occasionally. Immediately reduce heat to low. Simmer, uncovered and without stirring, for 10 minutes. Cool to room temperature. Pour syrup through a fine sieve into a container with a tight lid. Cover and refrigerate for up to 2 weeks.

Dark Chocolate Syrup

Great for milkshakes and sodas—even over ice cream or cake. If this syrup becomes too thick in the fridge, simply pop it in the microwave oven at HIGH for 20 to 30 seconds; stir before using. If you're using this syrup for a cold drink, don't let it get hot.

MAKES ABOUT 1½ CUPS

1¼ cups sugar
¾ cup unsweetened cocoa powder
⅛ tsp. salt
½ cup (4 oz.) water
½ cup (4 oz.) dark corn syrup
½ tsp. pure vanilla extract

In a medium, heavy saucepan, stir together sugar, cocoa powder, and salt. Slowly add water, then corn syrup, stirring until dry ingredients are moistened. Cook over medium-low heat, stirring constantly, until mixture comes to a boil. Reduce heat to low; cook, stirring often, for 3 minutes. Remove from heat. Cool to room temperature, stirring three or four times during that time. Stir in vanilla; cover and refrigerate for up to 1 month.

Ooey-Gooey Caramel Sauce

This *serious* caramel sauce makes magic in everything from hot drinks, like Hot Apple Pie, page 198, to chilly pleasers, like Caramel-Pecan Frostee, page 119. It's also a great sweetener for coffee and tea. For a more butterscotch flavor, substitute dark brown sugar for the light brown sugar.

MAKES ABOUT 2 CUPS

3 cups packed light brown sugar

¾ cup (6 oz.) heavy whipping cream

¾ cup (6 oz.) dark corn syrup

⅓ cup butter

⅛ tsp. salt

1½ Tbsp. (¾ oz.) pure vanilla extract

In a medium, heavy saucepan, combine all ingredients except vanilla. Cook over medium-high heat, stirring occasionally, until mixture reaches 230°F on a candy thermometer (or until a spoon coated with boiling syrup forms a 2-inch thread when dipped in a cup of cold water). Remove from heat; cool 30 minutes before stirring in vanilla. Cover and refrigerate for up to 2 weeks. To thin refrigerated sauce, microwave at HIGH for about 15 seconds; stir well.

Chocolate Whipped Cream

A decadent topping for chocolate and coffee drinks . . . heck, for almost anything at all!

MAKES ABOUT 2 CUPS

2 Tbsp. unsweetened cocoa powder
4 Tbsp. superfine sugar
1 cup (8 oz.) whipping cream
1 tsp. pure vanilla extract

In a small mixing bowl, stir together cocoa powder and sugar until thoroughly mixed. Slowly stir in whipping cream. Cover and refrigerate for 30 minutes. Beat cream until it forms soft mounds. Add vanilla; continue to beat until cream reaches desired consistency.

VARIATIONS

Mocha Whipped Cream   Add ½ Tbsp. instant espresso powder (or 1 Tbsp. instant coffee granules) to cocoa in first step; increase sugar by 2 Tbsp.

Coffee Whipped Cream   Substitute 2 Tbsp. instant espresso powder for the cocoa powder.

Toasted Coconut

Toasted coconut makes a wonderful garnish for drinks like Coconut-Mango Twister, page 108. Unsweetened, dried coconut is naturally sweet and can be found at Asian markets and natural food stores.

MAKES 1 CUP

1 cup unsweetened or sweetened shredded or
  flaked coconut

Preheat oven to 325°F. Spread coconut in a single layer on a baking sheet with shallow sides. Bake, tossing occasionally, for about 10 minutes, or until golden brown.

Vanilla Sugar

This delectably perfumed sugar can be substituted for plain old granulated sugar in myriad recipes.

MAKES 1 POUND

1 pound granulated, superfine, or powdered sugar
2 vanilla beans

In an airtight container, combine sugar and vanilla beans, pushing the beans well down into the sugar. Seal tightly; let stand for 1 to 2 weeks; give the container a shake two or three times during that period. The beans will flavor repeated batches of sugar; replenish the sugar as you use it. Replace the vanilla beans (or simply add new beans) every 4 to 6 months.

Punch-Bowl Ice

When buying a block of ice for a punch bowl, be sure it will fit your bowl and still leave room for the punch. If you can't find a block small enough, make your own punch-bowl ice the day before you need it. Simply fill an appropriate-size plastic or metal container (glass can crack when water expands) with water and freeze.

Ring molds (such as angel food cake or Bundt pans) make attractive punch-bowl ice, as do smaller decorative molds. For a novelty, balloons or latex (surgical) gloves may be used. Start by thoroughly rinsing out the balloons or gloves, then fill them with water and tie them closed *(very securely)*. Place the water-filled articles on a baking sheet and freeze. Before using, snip an edge of the balloon or glove and peel it off the ice.

Punch-bowl ice can be covered tightly and kept frozen for up to 2 weeks. To unmold, dip the bottom of the container in lukewarm water. Invert the mold and turn out the ice onto a piece of heavy-duty aluminum foil. Rewrap and place in the freezer until ready to use.

Flavored Ice Mold   Make extra punch and use it to fill the mold. Or use a sparkling beverage, such as ginger ale.

Colored Ice Mold   Add food coloring until the desired shade is achieved. Keep in mind that the melting ice will color the punch.

Decorated Ice Mold   Fill container half full with water; freeze until solid. Place fruit (grape clusters, pineapple rings, orange or lemon slices, etc.) or edible flowers (nonpoisonous and pesticide-free) on the surface of the ice. Carefully pour cold water (water that's been boiled and cooled is clearer than water directly from the tap) to cover the fruit; freeze until solid. If necessary, add more water to fill container to top and freeze.

Flavored Ice Cubes

The flavor of any iced drink will be less diluted if the ice cubes themselves are flavored. The flavoring depends on the drink to which the ice cubes will be added—**tomato-juice cubes** for Virgin Marys (page 249), **coffee cubes** for iced-coffee drinks, and so on. **Watermelon cubes** are showy and delicious. Purée seeded watermelon and combine with a little cold water to thin the mixture. Freeze in ice cube trays and add to drinks like Watermelon Whirl, page 60, or lemonades or spritzers. Prepare extra lemonade and make **lemonade cubes** with it ahead of time. The same goes for **punch cubes.**

The amount of liquid needed depends on the size of the ice cube tray—most hold from 10 to 14 regular-size cubes. Don't use miniature ice cube trays—the tiny cubes melt too fast.

MAKES ABOUT 12 REGULAR-SIZE ICE CUBES

1½ to 2 cups (12 to 16 oz.) liquid (fruit juice, coffee, tea, etc.)

Pour liquid into ice cube tray. Freeze for about 4 hours, or until firm.

VARIATIONS

Decorated Ice Cubes   Place a small piece of fruit (cherry, grape, melon ball, pineapple chunk, raspberry, lemon or orange twist, and so on) or an edible flower or flower petal (nonpoisonous and pesticide-free) in each section of an ice cube tray. Cover with cold water that has been boiled and cooled (it is clearer than water directly from the tap). Freeze until solid.

Frozen Fruit "Cubes"   Line a freezer-size baking sheet with plastic wrap; set aside. Cut fruit (melon, pineapple,

oranges, plums, papaya, etc.) into large 1- to 1½-inch
chunks or wedges; peeling is optional. Brush the cut
edges of fruit that darkens when exposed to air (like
peaches and apples) with lemon juice. Use fruit like
strawberries or grapes whole. Place fruit on prepared
baking sheet; freeze until solid, about 3 hours. Transfer
fruit from baking sheet to a freezer bag; freeze for up to
3 months.

Index

About the Author

Sharon Tyler Herbst, dubbed the foremost writer of user-friendly food and drink reference works, is an award-winning author of fourteen books. She gained her reputation as an accomplished culinary powerhouse with *The Food Lover's Companion,* broadly hailed as "a must for every cook's library." That volume and *The Wine Lover's Companion* (coauthored with her husband, Ron) are the online dictionaries for several major food and drink Internet sites. Julia Child praised Sharon's *Food Lover's Tiptionary* as "an invaluable help for all," and TV's popular quiz show *Jeopardy!* often cites Sharon's books as references. She is also a food and travel journalist, and a media personality whose myriad appearances on national radio and television shows include *Good Morning America* and the *Today* show. She's a consultant and spokesperson for national food and beverage companies and a past president of the International Association of Culinary Professionals (IACP). Her Internet site is *Food and Drink INK®* (sharontylerherbst.com).

Made in the USA
Middletown, DE
28 September 2015